W9-AUA-843

MERCEDES-BENZ 300SL

Osprey AutoHistory

MERCEDES-BENZ 300SL

Gull-wing & Roadster; 3 litre, 6 cylinder

WILLIAM BODDY

Published in 1983 by Osprey Publishing Limited
12–14 Long Acre, London WC2 9LP
Member company of the George Philip Group

Sole distributors for the USA

Motorbooks International
Publishers & Wholesalers Inc
Osceola, Wisconsin 54020, USA

British Library Cataloguing in Publication Data

Boddy, William
Mercedes-Benz 300SL.—(Autohistory)
1. Mercedes automobile
I. Title II. Series
629.2′222 TL215.M4

ISBN 0-85045-501-4

Editor Tim Parker
Associate Michael Sedgwick
Photography Mirco Decet
Design Behram Kapadia

Filmset in Great Britain
Printed in Spain
by Grijelmo S. A., Bilbao.

Contents

Introduction

Mercedes-Benz have long been known for top-quality motor cars and along the line, since Benz started making horseless-carriages in 1885, there have been many great sports models. One recalls the 60 hp Mercedes, which so nobly upheld the prestige of the German *marque* in the 1903 Gordon Bennett Race in Ireland after the intended Ninety team-cars had been destroyed in a fire at the factory. The Ninety itself was a car very much in the Edwardian sporting tradition, and was beloved by the young Count Louis Zborowski, to die driving a 2-litre straight-eight Mercedes—the make engraved not only on *his* ebullient heart but also on his father's—during the European Grand Prix at Monza in 1924. Then, in 1908, Mercedes won the classic French Grand Prix at Dieppe, Christian Lautenschlager's winning car followed home by two Benz, and in 1914 came that never-to-be-forgotten French Grand Prix at Lyon when, on the eve of war, three purposeful, white 4½-litre Mercedes came home in 1, 2, 3 order, having vanquished the might of Peugeot and other French makes.

The first experiments by Mercedes into super-charging for production cars, with the 10/40 hp model of 1921, led to those great, highly-covetable, now immortal, Dr Ferdinand Porsche-designed

Sports Mercedes—An 300SL Roadster parked with a classic 1928 SS model and two later cars, including a 540K

sports cars, the 33/180 hp, 36/220 hp and 38/250 hp Mercedes-Benz—any schoolboy's dream, and definitely mine!

This book is about a later generation of Mercedes-Benz sports-cars—the inimitable 300SL, best-known in 'gull-wing' coupé form, and its derivatives. Now a 'classic' automobile in its own right, a collector's motor car, this was a splendid example of the car from Stuttgart in its day, of which I have had some experience. Indeed, I have driven most Mercedes, from that veteran flier, the Sixty, to the current type 500SEC, and am a confirmed admirer. The 300SL was especially exciting because it marked the era of Mercedes-Benz' last entry into International motor racing, leading directly to those impeccable W196 Formula 1 single seaters and 300SLR straight-eight desmodromically-valved, fuel-injection team-cars which, among other successes, won the 1955 Mille Miglia, driven by Stirling Moss, and navigated by Denis Jenkinson, at an average speed of 97.96 mph.

It is not altogether surprising that Mercedes and Benz—the amalgamation dates from 1926—have

A galaxy of 300SLs. Racing version, prototype and production 300SL coupé grouped together with, foremost, the aggresive 300SLR coupé, of the kind used as a road car by Mercedes-Benz development engineer Rudi Uhlenhaut

had so many important competition successes and are responsible, in my humble opinion, for the best-engineered cars in the world—because Karl Benz was responsible for the very first motor car, his pioneer horseless-carriage, away back in 1885/86.

Whatever Mercedes-Benz of Stuttgart-Untertürkheim tackle, they do with characteristic thoroughness and style. Whether it was going motor racing, as with the 300SL and later 300SLR cars under the racing management of Herr Alfred Neubauer, presenting their cars at a motor show, or just bringing some pre-1905 veteran Mercedes and Benz to an RAC/VCC Brighton Run in this country, the transporters, the workforce, the Teutonic efficiency, and the undisguised enthusiasm and determination, are unwavering, and say it all. . . .

This book is about one, I hope enthralling, part of that magnificent whole.

Bill Boddy

Chapter 1
The lead in

Before the Second World War, as I have said, Mercedes and then Mercedes-Benz had built up an enviable reputation for winning very important motor races by a combination of engineering experience and skills and a blend of Teutonic efficiency and determination. I well remember the impression the arrival of the Mercedes-Benz cavalcade of transporters, workshop trucks and the fabulous racing cars themselves—the most powerful and fastest Grand Prix road racing machines in the world—made on me and other British observers, when they arrived at Donington Park in 1937, under the control of the legendary and inimitable Alfred Neubauer, with Rudi Caracciola, Dick Seaman, Manfred von Brauchitsch and Hermann Lang to drive them. The sounds these racing Mercedes made, their speed and acceleration, the pungent fumes from their exhausts, and the sheer efficiency of their preparation and operation, were quite out of the normal run of motor racing. So was the performance of these fabulous racing cars—I recall that when watching the first day's practice at Donington the late John Eason Gibson and I had the necessary track press-passes and stood beside the road, awaiting the appearance of Caracciola and Seaman as they emerged from the wooded part

Pre-war dual—Berndt Rosemeyer trying to get to grips in his oversteering Auto-Union with Rudi Caracciola's Mercedes-Benz at Donington Park

Top *Von Brauchitsch at speed out of a corner in a W163 Mercedes-Benz.*

Bottom *The dedicated and efficient Mercedes-Benz racing mechanics in action, electrically starting a Grand Prix car with their detachable starter-motor. Note the heavily-treaded tyres*

of the circuit in a crash of sound—as they approached we put prudence above curiosity and hastily climbed back over the protective fencing....

Although at first the new generation of Grand Prix Mercedes-Benz had teething troubles, allowing the rival AutoUnion team, both weapons in Herr Hitler's prewar Nazi publicity campaign, to win some of the races, soon Mercedes-Benz were dominant, and there is little doubt but that this earned them much credit around the world, which paid off after hostilities ceased in 1945.

Consequently, motor racing enthusiasts were ever anxious to see a resumption of racing by the incredible Mercedes-Benz engineers, the team controlled by the well-remembered Herr Neubauer. By 1951 the great Untertürkheim manufacturer had decided that the resumption of a racing programme would be useful, and it is said that a deputation

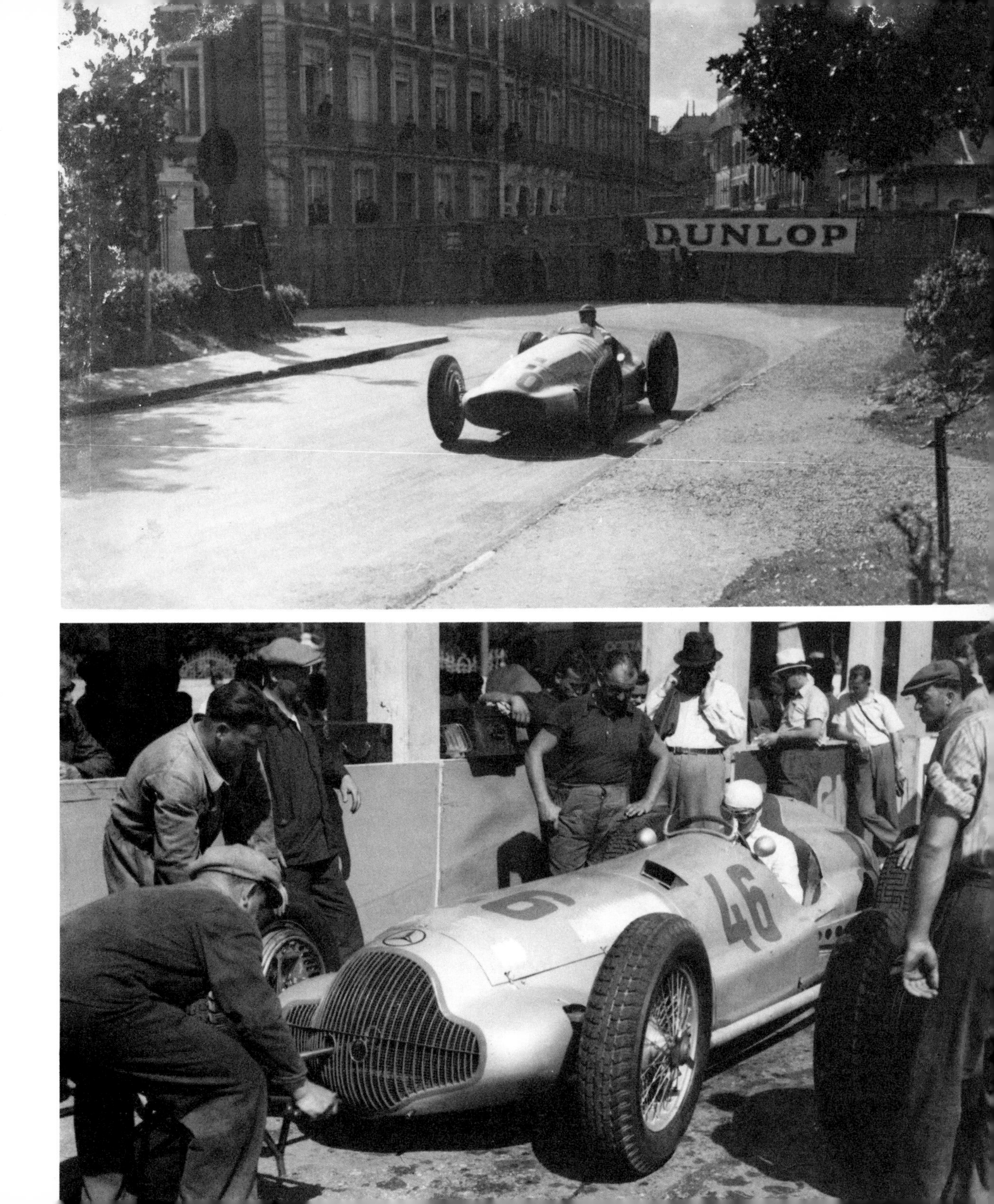
DUNLOP
46

consisting of Neubauer, ex-mechanic but later top racing driver Hermann Lang, and another Mercedes-Benz racing driver, Karl Kling, went to Le Mans, to watch that year's 24 hour sports-car race, won by Jaguar. On their return, and in conference with the Mercedes-Benz designer Franz Roller, they discussed how best the material embodied in existing Mercedes production models could be turned to good use on the international racing circuits, in the then strongly-represented sports-car events. It seems that others of the top-design group, like Ludwig Kraus and Manfred Lorscheidt, who worked under the great Rudy Uhlenhaut—who, in those prewar racing days just referred to, was well able to test the most powerful Mercedes-Benz Grand Prix cars, lapping almost as fast as the best drivers in the team and being able accurately to diagnose the causes of the symptoms he discovered—were attached to this team. Its purpose was to research the future of Mercedes-Benz on the sports-car market and in sports-car racing.

So what did they see, as they inspected the current range of cars in the making at Stuttgart and sifted through the drawings? They were looking at a prestigious sedan, on this visit to the passenger-car section of Daimler-Benz' Central Design Office, with a definite return to sports-car manufacture and motor racing as their objective. The car the team of engineers and former Daimler-Benz racing drivers concentrated on was the Type 300 Mercedes-Benz, a fine motor car using an 85×88 mm, six-cylinder 2996 cc engine with overhead-camshaft valve-gear, developing 115 bhp at 4600 rpm, on a compression-ratio of 6.4:1, that functioned effectively within the prevailing limitations of fuel and service conditions. This 300 engine had a cast-iron cylinder block, its forged steel crankshaft ran in seven main bearings, and it weighed 585 lb. The camshaft

Elegence of outline! A Mercedes-Benz 300S Roadster photographed under the nose of an aeroplane of the period. The girl driver wears a linen helmet, another period piece. Much of the technicalities of this car found their uses in the later 300SL

IAR
ROALD
AW27-3107

Top *The car for German executives of the 1950s—the Type 300 four-door sedan. Its tubular chassis and other components were the subject of an extensive technical study before the sports 300SL coupe was planned.*

was chain-driven, with a mechanically-adjusted tensioner-sprocket, and long finger-tappets were interposed between the cams and the valves, of which there were two for each cylinder, inclined at 20 degrees, the exhaust-valve stems being 3 mm greater in diameter than those of the inlet valves and filled with sodium salts for cooling. This ohc engine was used in a chassis having parallel-wishbone independent front suspension with coil-springs, and swing-axle independent rear suspension with the differential-unit mounted on the chassis frame, the springing medium being again by coil springs, supplemented by longitudinal torsion-bars, with an electrically-actuated self-levelling device incorporated.

The chassis frame which the aforesaid engineers were carefully inspecting was formed of oval-section tubes, cross-braced, and it was being made in two wheelbase lengths, 10 ft 0 in. for the saloons and 9 ft 6 in. for the more sporting models. Although there were distinct traces of Mercedes-Benz racing ancestry about this Type 300 production chassis, it was an improbable basis for a proper sporting car in the best traditions of Stuttgart. But the design-team ordered to work on the concept realized that it was that, or nothing. . . .

That was how, 32 years ago, work began on what was to become the most exciting and prestigious of postwar production Mercedes-Benz cars, the 300SL. So what was there that could be incorporated in the intended new models? Well, the chassis frame was regarded, with its substantial tubular side-members and 'X' cross-bracing, as too heavy and obviously the current Mercedes-Benz bodywork wasn't required. The front suspension units were, however, used with little alteration, except that the upper wishbones were drilled to reduce their weight, while the rear axle system was used almost as it

Bottom *The convertible version of the Tipo 300 Mercedes-Benz saloon was this Cabriolet D, still with four doors and a type of body the German coachbuilders did rather well, even if not contriving to make the hoods disappear, when these are not unfolded over the seats.*

stood, but with the elimination of the auxiliary torsion bars, and the shock-dampers were placed behind instead of in front of the swing axles.

It was the chassis which marked the break-through for the new 300SL cars. This became a specialized structure of a great many welded-up, small-bore steel tubes, to provide a stressed space-frame. It was notably strong in beam and torsion, yet not as heavy as a conventional chassis. This idea of using tubes assembled as a spaced structure to provide strength with light weight was not new. Lancia had used it for their now immortal Lambda model at the end of the First World War, its solidity enabling the Turin company to employ their well-known vertical sliding-strut, independent front springing. By 1951 the Mercedes-Benz engineers had seen Aston Martin, Cisitalia, Jaguar and others using space frames for their sports/racing cars, and Herr Rudolf Uhlenhaut had had previous experience of this kind of frame construction.

That evolved for the 300SL, or Type W194 as the Mercedes-Benz engineers knew the new car, had two large tubes, as cross-members front and back, these being united by a lattice-work of small-diameter steel tubes. The cross tubes served as mounting points for the front suspension units and the frame-mounted differential casing, respectively. The idea was that such a multiple-tube space-frame would carry only tension and compression loads, and be exceptionally light for the weight of steel incorporated. However, there was one necessity, which was to give the celebrated 300SL Mercedes-Benz much of its character. This was that, to achieve the necessary stiffness, the frame tubes had to run beside the cockpit openings, where side doors are provided on ordinary cars. This problem was overcome by fitting upwards- and outwards-opening 'gull-wing' doors (as we shall see later, upwards- and forwards-opening flaps sufficed on subsequent open-

Some of those responsible for Mercedes-Benz supremacy. Left to right: *Herr Neubauer, the racing manager; Hermann; engineer Uhlenhaut; W. I. Tak; our Peter Collins, seated; Engel; Taruffi; Kling; Fangio; Graf von Trips; Stirling Moss and Gendebien of the race circuits; Simon; Frauline Thiron, with bouquet; Fitch, Herr-Director von Baden-Wurttemberg; Dr. Veit and engineer Nallinger, Taruffi is demonstrating the race-dominating aspects of the postwar GP Mercedes-Benz, of which the 300SLR sports-racer was a sister under the skin*

bodied 300SL cars, to comply with competition requirements). This construction also meant that driver and passenger were obliged to step down over a considerable sill, into the seats of this Mercedes model—bashful females to note!

It should be made clear that this chassis design was for coupé bodywork, regarded as giving the best aerodynamic low-drag characteristics and providing beneficial comfort for driver and mechanic in long sports-car races. At first they were concerned about achieving easy access to the difficult-to-attain cockpit and set a step into the body side, but after 1952 this was omitted from the production drawings.

The tubular frame was designed by Franz Roller's office. They used tubing that formed a point ahead of the cockpit bulkhead to absorb front-end stresses; by the centre line of the car a braced ring of double tubes went around the body. Aft, boxed trusses ran to a bulkhead behind the seats, and more small-diameter tubes ran upwards to the rear cross-member, continuing rearwards to support the fuel tank and two spare wheels, the latter angled outwards at, and above, the back face of the tank.

LE CIMENT ARME

There'r off! Before packed grandstands the Mercedes-Benz of Juan Manual Fangio and Karl Kling lead the field at the start of the 1954 French Grand Prix at Reims, over a course constructed of tarmacadam. They finished in that order, Fangio winning at 115.67 mph for the 311.21-mile race. Manzon's Ferrari was third, building up prestige for the 300SL sports car

For racing purposes a very sleek aluminium panelled coupé body was designed by the Sindelfingen drawing office, the skilled work of Karl Wilfert and others, who contrived to keep the frontal area down to a useful 19.4 square feet, resulting in a highly-commendable drag-coefficient of 0.25. Instead of a stark cockpit, reminiscent of a present-day 'works' sports/racing car or a formidable rally-car, Mercedes-Benz upholstered the interior of these race-intended 300SL coupés to high standards, in a plaid-cloth trim, believing that this would enhance the endurance of their chosen drivers.

The wheelbase of these new Mercedes-Benz racing coupés measured 7 ft 10½ in. and the rear track was one of 4 ft 8.9 in., the front track being 4 ft 6.4 in. It was decided to retain the standard wheel size of 15 in. used on the production Mercedes-Benz 300 cars, and after a spell on bolt-on wheels, the 300SL was provided with centre-lock hubs for its disc wheels, the light-alloy rims of which were shod with 6.70 × 15 Continental tyres.

The brakes presented something of a problem and a compromise. Disc brakes were being used in racing by 1951/52, but the Mercedes designers decided to use drum brakes, in spite of their weight. What they did was to use Al-Fin cast-iron/light alloy drums, the same 260 mm diameter as used on the catalogue Mercedes-Benz 300 cars, but wider, and equipped with turbine-type cooling fins. The front brakes were of the two-leading-shoe pattern, those at the rear being of the leading- and trailing-shoe type. The linings came from Great Britain, in the form of Ferodo VG95 material, cemented to the alloy shoes.

That was the car into which the new power-unit was to go. The complexity of the space frame meant that the engine had to be inclined, at 50 degrees from the vertical, towards the left or near-side of the

Tight fit! Two Grand Prix Mercedes-Benz packed into their racing transporter

car. It was also off-set several inches towards the off-side of the frame. At first they tried to dispense with dry-sump lubrication, using an oversize alloy sump, but it wasn't long before a change was made to a dry sump, in conjunction with the normal ploy of putting a scavenging pump below the pressure oil-pump. To make the sparking plugs easier to fit and remove with the inclined engine new cylinder heads were designed, the plugs then living in the heads and not in the cylinder block.

Special pistons raised the compression-ratio to 8.0:1, but valve sizes were unchanged from those of the 300 limousines in which affluent German citizens were wont to commute. The camshaft was revised, however, and three Solex carburetters were fitted, so naturally there were some changes in the exhaust piping. The engine now delivered 171 bhp at 5200 rpm as used for normal sports/racing car events, and according to the authority on Mercedes-Benz racing, Karl Ludvigsen, the safe revolutions per minute were 5800, with 6400 sometimes used in anger. At 4200 rpm maximum torque, 188 lb ft, was developed.

It wasn't until late in 1951 that the 300SL or W194 coupé was available for testing. Herr Neubauer was naturally in full charge, and he did not like what he saw. More power, better brakes, larger tyres and a five-speed gearbox were demanded by the portly, forthright team manager.

Chapter 2
Mercedes-Benz returns to racing

Had Neubauer not been insistent, the Daimler-Benz Herr-Directors might have stifled any desire to resume their former 'invincible' programme of racing, if only because the resources of Untertürkheim were absorbed in meeting the demand for their top-quality, splendidly-engineered production cars. It is thought that Rudi Uhlenhaut prevailed upon the irascible racing manager to keep a low profile at this time, the chief engineer, it has been said, believing that the 300SL could match, even vanquish, British and Italian sports/racing cars which weighed less and developed about 30 bhp more.

The result of whatever transpired was that Daimler-Benz resumed racing work by entering a team of W194s for Rudi Caracciola, Karl Kling, and Hermann Lang—none of them exactly youthful exponents of the art of driving powerful racing cars—in the famous Mille Miglia 1000 mile Italian road-race. There was considerable prestige at stake, and all who rooted for the cars wearing the illustrious three-pointed star must have been near-hysterical when the ageing, silver-haired Karl Kling led into the Rome control, from the classic dive off the starting-ramp in Brescia. Alas, it had been said that he who led at Rome never won this

long, fast, punishing contest. Kling was strongly challenged by Giovanni Bracco in a 3-litre V12 Ferrari, but Bracco had been held back by tyre troubles. Lang was already out, his Mercedes-Benz having collided with a roadside obstacle, and the once-great Caracciola had started with an engine of less power than those in the other two 300SLs, perhaps from lack of time to prepare anything better. After Rome, Bracco forged ahead, driving without a relief driver, in a manner either mad or brilliant, depending on one's personal view. He won a very popular victory for Enzo Ferrari, finishing 4

The first of the revolutionary 300SL gull-wing coupés prepared for the 1952 sports-car races. Note the properly-upholstered seats

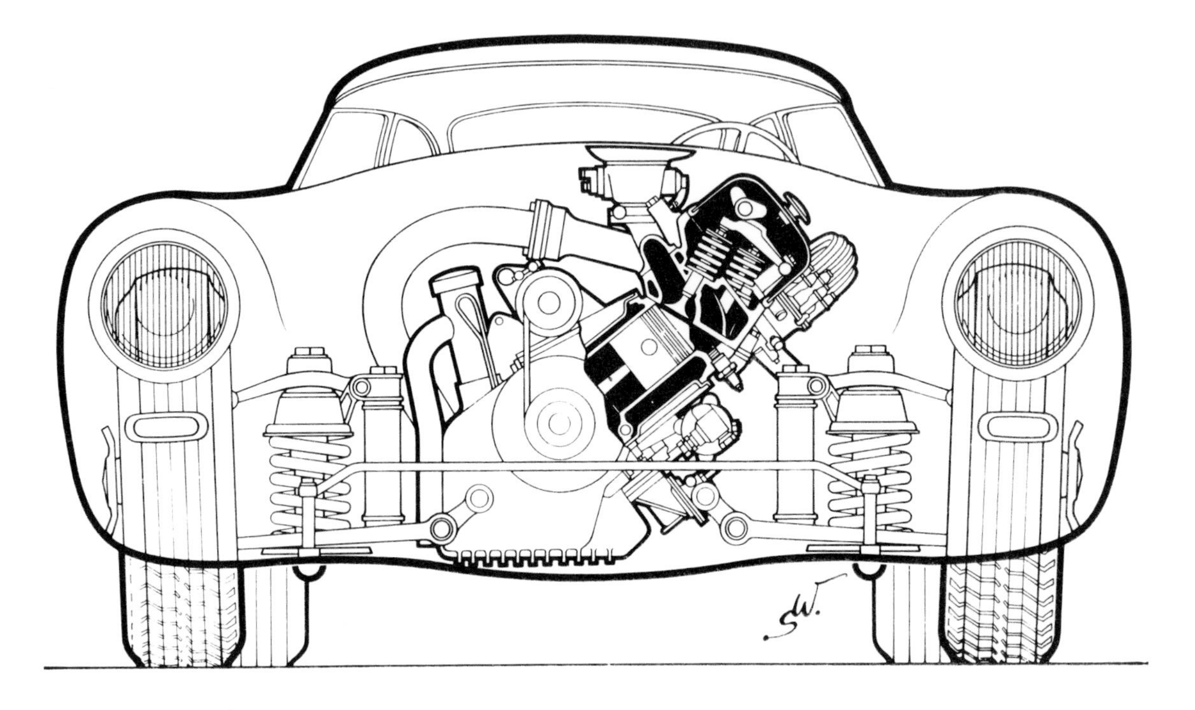
SW.

min 32 sec ahead of Kling, with Luigi Fagioli third in a Lancia Aurelia. Caracciola was fourth. Not perhaps an over-auspicious start but Daimler-Benz were back in the game they had so often dominated, for to them competing was synonymous with winning. . . .

The next appearance of these shapely, sleek 300SL coupés was in the sports-car contest that preceeded the Swiss Grand Prix at Bern—once the preserve of victorious GP Mercedes single-seaters. Four cars were there, a spare, and the race-entries for Caracciola, Kling, and Lang, with the spare car, equipped with doors that looked a bit more like doors (ready for Le Mans scrutineering comment!) raced by Fritz Reiss. Sadly, this was Caracciola's last race—he was a victim of brake lock-on which Kling had coped with during the Mille Miglia, and after three crashes, he decided to retire, his 300SL slamming into a tree on this occasion. However, the Bern race was a 1, 2, 3 victory (Kling, Lang, Reiss) for Mercedes.

Le Mans was the next, and very important, engagement for the coupés from Stuttgart. Three new cars were built specially for the French 24-hour night-and-day marathon. Kling was to be partnered by Hans Klenk, who had ridden with him in the noisy, hot cockpit of the Mille Miglia winner, Lang with Reiss, and Theo Helfrich and Norbert Niedermayer (who?) had the third Mercedes-Benz. Before the race Uhlenhaut and his team of engineers experimented with air brakes, on the roof of the spare car. The idea worked as far as powerful retardation was concerned, but the roof-pylons proved unequal to the drag and the scheme was abandoned—I remember Denis Jenkinson remarking how, when preparation of the later 300SLR sports/racing cars was under discussion, there was little that was new or experimental in the Daimler-Benz book, or rather, it was all entered, from

Top *Breakaway drawings showing how the major front-end components of the 300SL coupé were laid out. The engine, as is clear, was steeply inclined to the near-side, with the insuction trunk on the right, and front suspension is by coil springs*

Bottom *What you saw of the complex 300SL power-pack in the engine-bay of this exciting motor-car*

613
W59-4999

previous experiments, in their technical notes!

With engines detuned by approximately five horsepower to safeguard reliability, the team arrived in France with all the signs of the advanced planning and military-like cavalcade that I recall from witnessing the arrival of these fabulous W125 and W154 Mercedes Grand Prix teams at Donington in 1937 and 1938, as described in the *Motor Sport* book about racing at the Derbyshire circuit. Now in 1952 there was another highly impressive Mercedes-Benz cavalcade to an important motor race. Mercedes had their troubles, but Neubauer in the end had the satisfaction of winning, as intended. It was the year when that unlucky Frenchman, Pierre Levegh, saw victory within his grasp, refused to let

Line-up of the Mercedes-Benz 300SL team for the race at Berne, Switzerland, in 1952. Note the altered doors of the last car in the row, to comply with the Le Mans regulations

Left *An evocative photograph of a 300SL taken during the 1952 Mille Miglia race*

Mercedes-Benz are sound technicians above everything, and for Le Mans in 1952 this air-brake was tried out in practice, although not used on the 300SLs in the race

Bottom—*Exciting moment; the Mercedes line-up at Le Mans, with the sleek new coupés ready to go*

anyone else drive the $4\frac{1}{2}$-litre Talbot-Lago on which the hopes of France and all the French spectators rested, and, fatigued towards the close of his long stint, missed a gear change and felt a connecting rod break. Lang and Reiss forged ahead to win Le Mans at a record average speed of 96.67 mph, with the Helfrich/Niedermayer Mercedes in second place, at an average speed of 95.67 mph, the respective milages they had covered in the 24 hours being 2320.3 and 2311.8. Third place was taken by a 4.1-litre Nash-Healey; the third of the 3-litre 300SLs had retired with failure of its Bosch dynamo.

On their way to victory. Two of the 300 SL coupés cornering during the 1952 Le Mans marathon

W83-3146

To set this return-to-racing in perspective, in 1951 the Le Mans race had been won by the Walker/Whitehead 3.4-litre Jaguar XK120C (C type) at 93.498 mph, and in 1953 it was to be a victory for the Rolt/Hamilton Jaguar of this type, at 105.85 mph. So the silver-hued Mercedes-Benz coupés had proved their worth early in their career—alas, when Daimler-Benz gave Levegh a drive in a 300SLR at Le Mans in 1955, as we shall see, it ended in a holocaust, and the death of the keen and courageous French driver.

The next racing engagement for the 300SLs was the shorter sports/racing car contest on home ground, over the twisting, difficult Nürburgring in August. With typical appreciation of the situation, Mercedes prepared new cars at Sindelfingen for this

The sleek lines of the 300SL Roadster, in the form in which it was raced in the Eifel race

Top left *Frontal view of the open-bodied Mercedes fitted with a supercharged engine. John Fitch drove it in the PanAmerica race*

Bottom *Consultation at the Nürburgring in 1952. Herr Neubauer on extreme right. Uhlenhaut has been driving during a test-session, Karl Bung has the door ready to refit, Ludwig Krams (in shirt and tie) stands behind him*

In line formation, the 300SLs at the Nürburging in 1952

21
22

very different kind of race, because it had been decided that light weight was important. The coupés were converted into open-bodied roadsters, by chopping-off the cockpit tops. The exhaust pipe was shortened, emerging from the off-side ahead of the back axle, and it is even said that all the instruments formerly on the dashboard were removed, except for oil-pressure and water temperature gauges. Thus was born the 300SL Roadster.

Three of these cars were former coupés, altered as just outlined, and two of them the Le Mans cars, but Kling had a brand-new Roadster, with a wheelbase of 7 ft 2.7 in. and a different radiator-grille. What is more, experiments were conducted with supercharging the 3-litre six-cylinder engine, but the swing-axle rear suspension proved to be the limiting factor and the idea was abandoned. The race was won by Lang, with Kling second, after he had lost his lead to his team-mate due to an oil leak from his car getting onto the rear tyres. The Reiss/Helfrich Mercedes was third.

That was virtually the end of the 300SL, as a coupé and a roadster, on the race circuits. Daimler-Benz, gratified by their return to the competition world, decided to concentrate on building another team of true Grand Prix, Formula One racing cars, which are outside the scope of this book.

However, there was to be a final fling. It centred around the Mexico City Road Race, a five-day, November grind of nearly 2000 miles. Although notice was short, entirely typically Mercedes fielded a three-car team, and Ludvigsen has said that they advanced into Mexico with two $3\frac{1}{2}$-ton transporters, a spare race-car, some 35 racing *personnel*, and 300 tyres of various kinds. The scheme was to race two coupé 300SLs, one a Le Mans car, the other largely assembled from the wreck of Caracciola's accident at Bern, and a Roadster, with a spare Roadster to be driven by

journalist Gunther Molter following the race-stages. As there was no 3-litre class at Mexico, the engine-size was increased to 3.1-litres, gaining an extra six bhp, and full-width windscreens were fitted to the Roadsters. Opposition was stiff in this very tough and demanding Carrera Panamericana, particularly from the new 4.1-litre Ferraris and the far-from-slow Gordinis.

A publicity picture, judging by the numberplate, of the 300SL coupé entered for the 1952 Carrera-PanAmerica road race, a tough struggle in which Mercedes triumphed

Mercedes had tyre trouble to contend with and Lang's 135 mph coupé hit a dog and Kling a buzzard that crashed through the windscreen with a loud report. The cars from Stuttgart had, however, conserved their full effort for the later stages of the race, in accordance with Neubauer's plan, and it paid off. Incidentally, M-B organization went as far

as Neubauer watching Kling outpacing the spotter aeroplane in which the racing manager had been trying to keep an eye on his drivers in rally fashion! After a change to a higher axle-ratio before the last stages, Kling won at an astonishing 102.359 mph, Lang backing him up in second place, at 99.274 mph, with Chinetti's bigger Ferrari third, after Bracco's had succumbed to differential failure. The Mercedes cars triumphed in this brutal battle, though their bodies were torn, dented, pock-marked, and the paint sand-blasted, before they completed the course. Fitch/Geiger were disqualified, through using outside assistance to re-align the front wheels of their Mercedes.

The racing return of Daimler-Benz can be summarized thus:

Victory in the hard-fought 1952 Carrera-PanAmerican race for the 300SL, dependent to some extent on Mercedes strategy

Mille Miglia	2nd Kling; 4th Caracciola
Bern	1st Kling; 2nd Lang; 3rd Reiss
Le Mans	1st Lang/Reiss; 2nd Helfrich/Niedermayer
Nürburgring	1st Lang; 2nd Kling; 3rd Reiss/Helfrich
Carrera Panamericana	1st Kling; 2nd Lang

Those were the only official race-engagements and this is a formidable result indeed, for a first season with new cars, and the first return of Mercedes-Benz to racing since before the war. I just hope that anyone still running a 300 sedan is proud of its contribution to such a convincing and magnificent season. . . .

Chapter 3
The production model 300SL

Although the Daimler-Benz directors had thought to withdraw from racing almost as soon as they had so successfully resumed this pursuit, by August 1952 in fact, and only went to race in Mexico that November because Herr Neubauer prevailed upon them so to do, development of the 300SL had been continuing, in readiness for the 1953 competition season that was to be still-born.

More power had been extracted from the 3-litre six-cylinder engine by replacing the Solex carburetters with Webers. The gain at first was a significant 11 bhp, increased to a useful 201 bhp at 5800 rpm after a re-designed cylinder head and bigger inlet valves and ports (diameter up by 2 mm, to 44 mm) had been incorporated. Torque was now up too, at 202 lb ft. That was one improvement. The chassis had not been overlooked. To enhance the road-holding (a swing-axle at the rear was bound to give oversteer in high speed cornering) a low-pivot assembly was introduced, a solution Volkswagen were to use in the same context, Mercedes having radius-arms to locate the hubs. At last 16 in. tyres were adopted, and the gull-wing body was cleaned up, to reduce weight, and give a 9 per cent smaller frontal area.

That was satisfactory, but Daimler-Benz were not

Top *Side elevation of a 1953 300SL, showing to perfection the side grilles and the gull-wing doors which will make this model forever recognisable and famous!*

Bottom *Frontal aspect of the same car, showing the prominent three-pointed star badge on uhe radiator grille and the recessed headlamps, which are quite small*

content to rest there. As I have previously remarked, this pioneer automobile manufacturer had most aspects of the art already tested and recorded. Fuel injection had been investigated 18 years earlier and now it was to be applied to the 300SL's power unit, under the auspices of Fritz Nallinger, with day-to-day development led by Heinz Lamm. Direct fuel-injection was found to lift the power of the 300SL engine to 208 bhp at 5700 rpm, or to 214 bhp with the larger inlet valves.

There further development of the 300SL might have been abandoned, had not there been a demand for a sporting Mercedes-Benz model for the American market. An order for 1000 such SL coupés from the New York Mercedes importer, Max Hoffman, was not to be denied. It is said that he got his way, a prototype of what was to become the production—

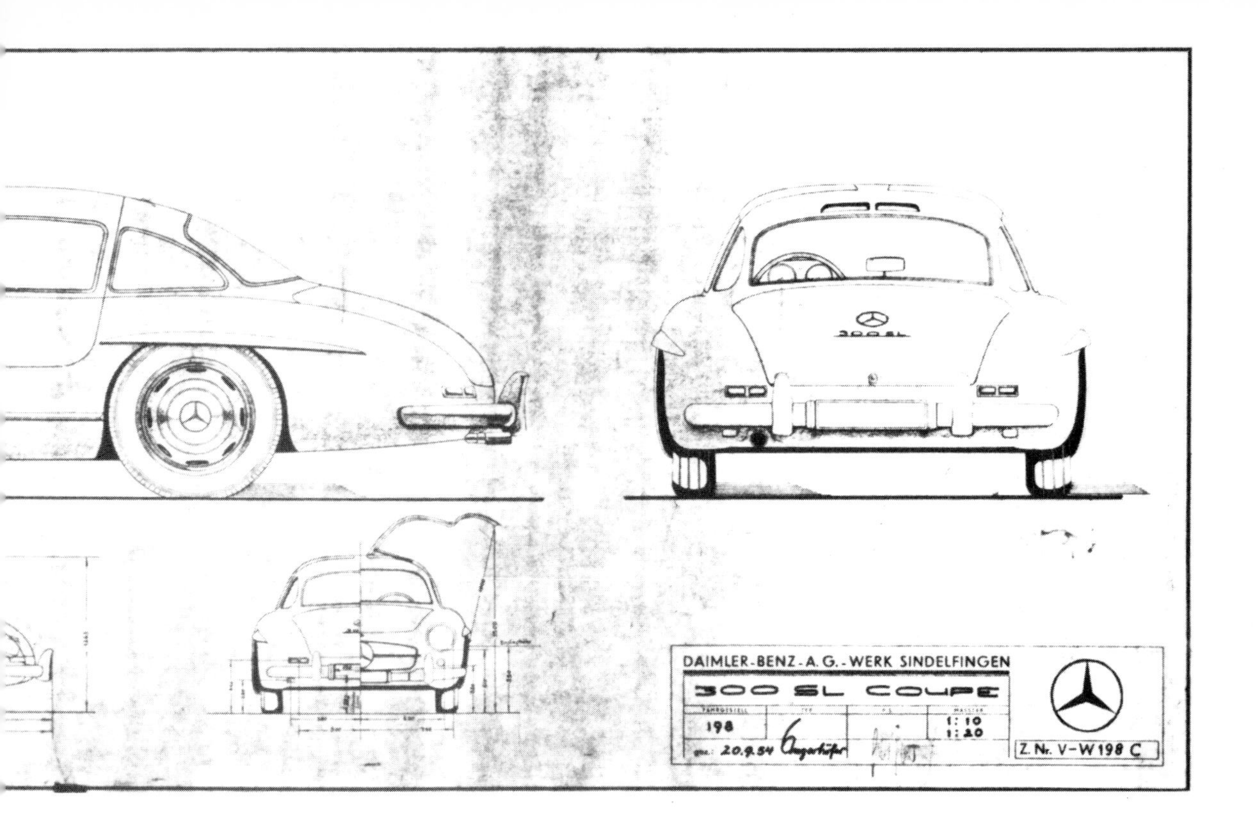

A works drawing of the body styling of the 300SL gull-wing coupé

the catalogued version—of the 300SL gull-wing coupé, the greatest of the postwar sporting Mercedes-Benz cars, being ready in January 1954.

Naturally, various refinements were incorporated, to prepare this very fast, race-bred, and exciting Mercedes for the motoring public, who would represent a discerning sector of the market for high-performance prestige motor-cars. Means were provided for properly heating and ventilation of the interior, although it has been said that the 300SL coupé was never easy to ventilate. Styling changes were introduced to the body that had been drawn by Paul Braiq under the direction of Karl Wilfert, and it was then that the twin bulges in the top of the bonnet-panel—to clear the cambox cover and the plenum chamber of the fuel-injection air-intake—appeared.

One notable development related to the remarkable new injection system for the engine, consisting of that long aluminium trunk, with the throttle-valve in its nose, and with down-pipes leading to the six individual 17 in. diameter intakes for the valve ports, from the plenum chamber, for the fuel-injection system developed in conjunction with the Bosch company. The production edition of the competition Mercedes-Benz 300SL had not been quite finaliszd when it made its debut, in February 1954, at the New York International Motor Show. It retained the 7 ft $10\frac{1}{2}$ in. wheelbase of the racing version but the front track was now 4 ft 6.6 in. and the rear track was 4 ft. $8\frac{1}{2}$ in. Changes in the ingenious space-frame, necessitated by the alterations to the bodywork, put its weight up by 181 lb and the production 300SL scaled 2552 lb, or about 2880 lb ready to motor, with the very large capacity (34.3 gallon) tank full of petrol. The recirculating-ball steering gear from the Mercedes-Benz 300 saloon replaced the ZF worm-and-nut steering gear used on the earlier cars. Although the cars at the New York Show were on racing Dunlops, the appearance of the 300SL coincided with the realisation that automobile manufacturers should work with the tyre makers in producing tyres suited to the suspension and performance characteristics of a given car. So Mercedes-Benz and Continental got together, and the 300SL was delivered on 6.70×15 Continental tyres on $5\frac{1}{2}$K rims. To aid the driver, a vacuum-servo was incorporated in the braking system.

That was how the 300SL coupé made its debut to the public. Enthusiasts with sufficiently full wallets had eagerly awaited it, even if entry and exit were unusual, luggage space extremely restricted, and driving it properly and effectively no easy task. A further disadvantage for British customers was that because of the inclined power unit, the 300SL was

The inimitable bodywork of the 300SL gull-wing coupé Mercedes-Benz was the responsibility of the Singelfingen factory. A 1954 model is seen outside this impressive works

only available with left-hand steering. But to those who could afford this beautiful, extremely fast and accelerative Mercedes-Benz these things mattered little, or not at all. Soon the new 300SL, officially a Type M198, with the Type W198 power-unit, was causing much interest and excitement all over the World.

English journalists had their first taste of the sort of motoring the 300SL could provide when tests were arranged for us at Silverstone circuit on 14 October, 1954. Rudolf Uhlenhaut drove selected motoring writers round the track, using the full main circuit, and later we were permitted to do a few fast laps ourselves. The car used was regarded as a demonstration hack; and it used the first of the

CHAPTER THREE

A new 300SL ready for its lucky owner. Note index mark and bumpers

production fuel-injection engines and was on Dunlop tyres. To give an impression of how the 300SL was regarded, in the context of the time, 29 years ago, I am quoting my report written after I had sampled this very impressive new Mercedes-Benz.

'The 300SL Mercédès-Benz, which created such a sensation in sports-car racing two years ago, until the manufacturers withdrew it from competitions because "they had learnt all they needed to know," was brought to Silverstone on October 14th for the delectation of a few favoured motoring journalists.

'Rudolf Uhlenhaut, head of the Mercédès-Benz experimental and racing department, drove each journalist for two or three fast laps of the full Silverstone circuit. This was a wonderful experience, for Uhlenhaut is well known to be nearly as fast as Fangio when it comes to poking a Mercédès round the circuits, and while he may have kept just a little in hand during these demonstration runs, the 300SL was driven very fast indeed, using all the available space on the corners. Uhlenhaut used only top and third gears, bringing the car out of the corners by skilful opening of the throttle, the speed rising to something like 112 m.p.h. along the straights.

'Later came the opportunity of trying the 300SL for oneself and while fast "lappery" masks rather than clarifies impressions of a strange car; especially one of this power and speed, we were impressed by the manner in which 6,000 r.p.m. came up in the indirect gears, equal to nearly 100 m.p.h. in third, the comfort and support of the cloth-upholstered bucket driving seat, the high-geared, taut, somewhat heavy steering, the very fine road-holding, swing-axle rear i.s. notwithstanding, and particularly by the great power of the light-to-apply, completely fade-free brakes, with their turbo-finned drums. Naturally, the extreme power and urge of the 300SL impressed. It also created favourable

comment for the manner in which it stood up to this continual high-speed without falter, the exhaust showing neither blue haze nor black smoke, the engine starting promptly, and no trouble of any sort remotely thought of, except for a big nail which punctured one of the Dunlops, although this car, with the first production fuel-injection engine, was used as a road-hack and probably did nearly 200 miles of fast work at Silverstone. The accelerator has a short travel and when it is depressed the result is interesting! The car snaked somewhat when taking an adverse camber and it is possible that a de Dion back-end would hold it down better, although it is certainly an outstandingly stable and safe car.

America represented an important export market for Mercedes-Benz and this is how the 300SL, appealing to blue-blooded sportsmen, was transported from the docks to New York, by Mercedes-Benz Distributors, Inc. of 443, Park Avenue

'It is a truly delectable motor-car and not surprisingly costs £4,392 15s. 10d. in this country, in spite of the fact that Mercédès have studied cost-reduction and hence use bolt-on wheels, drum brakes and a sheet steel body, etc. Although the price is high, there is, they appreciate, a limit, even for sales to the U.S.A.

'The instrument panel is in the modern, even ornate style, with quite modest speedometer and rev.-counter dials before the driver who, in this l.h.d. example, had a hand-brake lever on the left of his seat and a central remote gear-lever, nicely placed and controlling a gearbox with admirable synchromesh. Entry and egress to the two-seater cockpit with its luggage shelf behind the seats entails cocking the legs to negotiate the deep chassis sill, as the spring-loaded lift-up "Le Mans" doors are used, but head-room as you enter or emerge is unrestricted, as the doors form part of the roof. This construction is essential if a properly-stiff chassis frame is to be employed without a heavy weight-penalty; the frame is, indeed, formed of 25 mm. by 1 mm. "bicycle" tubes. The sliding windows seem rather small but visibility is excellent and head-room ample, whilst the luggage-boot is capacious.

'Mercédès-Benz are building 25 of these 300SL cars a month at present, selling mainly to America, and will soon increase production to 50 a month. They aim to build 500 in all, so that the car qualifies to race in the *Gran Turismo* class.

'The engine is a development of the 300 and 300S six-cylinder overhead camshaft 85 by 88 mm., 2,996 c.c. unit. With direct fuel injection, which, from our remarks above, it must be obvious that Stuttgart has got absolutely "taped," the power output is 212 b.h.p. at the clutch, using a compression-ratio of 8.55 to 1. We write "at the clutch" advisedly, for American enthusiasts get 240 b.h.p. by removing

An invitation to an exciting day's motoring perhaps? The gull-wing door on the passenger's side of the 300SL coupé, showing its contours and the handle for pulling it shut. Girls sometimes found it needed care to negotiate the sill of the bodywork gracefully!

cooling fan, exhaust mufflers and such like impediments. The b.m.e.p. is 158.5 lb./sq. in.

'The engine peaks at 5,800 r.p.m., but is safe up to 6,000 r.p.m. and will tolerate 6,400 r.p.m. in top gear if the low-ratio back axle is fitted.

'Uhlenhaut explained that Mercédès-Benz have adopted fuel-injection because it provides the same strength mixture in each cylinder, so that a higher compression-ratio can be employed than is possible with normal carburation, when the limiting factor is that of the leanest cylinder. The car we tried was using pump National Benzole and S.A.E. 20 Mobiloil. It shows not the slightest tendency to "pink." Besides this advantage of fuel injection, this system provides excellent low-speed torque, from 400 r.p.m. upwards, and makes the engine easier to operate under cosmopolitan conditions, inasmuch as jets do not require changing at high altitudes, as the fuel pump is provided with bellows for automatic altitude adjustment and also has automatic temperature and cold-start adjustments.

'Dirt is the enemy of the fuel-pump, as it is of a diesel-injection pump, but a double filter obviates most of the trouble. The only shortcomings of fuel-injection have been difficult hot-starting, cured by using an electric auxiliary pump to prime the system with cool fuel, and a tendency to "hunt," which however is confined to idling speeds and will be cured. A long induction pipe, feeding air to the inlet valves, damps out induction pulsations.

'The cost of fuel-injection is approximately £60 greater than that of normal carburation, but later on Mercédès-Benz will probably adopt it for their lower-priced cars.

'The 300SL will be available in open as well as coupé form next spring, but not as a four-seater, as Stuttgart consider such addition of weight quite out of keeping with their conception of a *Gran Turismo* motor car.

The gentleman, for such we hope he is, hopefully suggests a run in his 300SL to the lady, telling her, perhaps, that it is the fastest production car of its time

AW 27-20011

'Three different back axle ratios are available, 3.68 to 1 for normal touring, giving a maximum speed of 150 m.p.h., as used on the car we drove, 3.42 to 1, which provides a maximum of 155 m.p.h. and 3.25 to 1, which gives an all-out speed of 160 m.p.h.—quite a sports car! Using the "town" gear-ratios 40 m.p.h. is possible in first gear, 67 m.p.h. in second gear and 95 m.p.h. in third gear of the four-speed gearbox, but the higher axle ratio gives 75 m.p.h. in second gear and 107 m.p.h. in third. The weight of the coupé, ready to drive and full of fuel, is given as 25.5 cwt., suggesting a dry weight of about 23 cwt. Were a light-alloy body used some 80 kilo. could be saved, but the price would increase.

'Fuel consumption is quoted by Uhlenhaut as 44 m.p.g. at 30 m.p.h., 38 m.p.g. at 40 m.p.h., 35 m.p.g. at 60 m.p.h. constant speeds, the average range being between 14.8 and 24 m.p.g. for fast driving, including Alpine work. Uhlenhaut said that motoring "as fast as you can travel on British roads," including town-driving, the 300SL returns 18 to 20 m.p.g., a very conservative consumption for a 3-litre car of this kind, proving that low weight and a good aerodynamic form pay dividends here.

'For sports-car racing Mercédès-Benz have the new straight-eight 3-litre fuel-injection 300 SLR.

'Uhlenhaut said that next year this car will run in the important sports-car races and they hope to vanquish Ferrari, and Lancia if the latter *marque* runs. Open and closed versions of the 300SLR will be produced, but it is expected that the drivers will prefer the open cars for races like the Mille Miglia, because of the problem of keeping clean the windscreen of a coupé.

'Disc brakes are being investigated at Stuttgart, but will not necessarily be used. Already tests of a German-supplied Chrysler disc brake have been completed and Uhlenhaut now places high hopes in the Dunlop disc brake.

This is a classic among publicity pictures of the gull-wing 300SL, sent out when these were new cars, from the archives of Daimler-Benz Aktiengesellschaft

'He welcomes the increasing competition in Grand Prix racing and looks forward to 1955, when the sports/racing 300SLR will make its debut and the Mercédès-Benz G.P. cars are expected to be faster than they were this year.'

Already Uhlenhaut was using a 300SL as personal transport, and by 1955 the world's renowned motoring writers had given their personal views about this great Mercedes-Benz sports-car. Before it had been fully released in Europe, however, the American market had opened up and the 300SL began to re-appear in competition events in the hands of private owners, who were offered optional extras, such as centre-lock instead of the normal bolt-on wheels, and the sports camshaft which gave an extra 0.6 mm lift for the exhaust valves (from 7.8 mm) and which opened the inlet valves 2 degrees earlier, closing them 2 degrees sooner, and the exhaust valves 19 degrees earlier, closing them 7 degrees later. All 300SL engines were regarded as safe up to 6000 rpm for continuous operation and to 6400 rpm when it was required to be fully extended.

Even after the official racing programme with the 300SLR sports/racing cars and the W196 Grand Prix Mercedes was abandoned, with, it may be said, Daimler-Benz again invincible, the service to those racing their private 300 SL cars was continued, with some of the race-mechanics looking after their requirements, under the direction of Karl Bunz, with Kling, and even the great Neubauer, attending the more important events.

Among outstanding performances under these conditions can be sited the 5th place and a class win at 87 mph of Fitch and Gendebien in the 1955 Mille Miglia, victory in the Liège-Rome-Liège Rally by Olivier Gendebien, who also had a clear run in the Alpine Rally, victory in the Tulip Rally by W. I. Tak, and Werner Engel's European Touring Car Championship, Armando Zampiero's Italian sports-car-drivers' championship, and the American driver Paul O'Shea's SCCA class championship, all achieved with gull-wing 300SLs. In addition, several 300SL coupés competed in the 1955 Spanish sports-car Grand Prix, and these successes continued into 1956, with Prince Metternich finishing 6th in the Mille Miglia, Shock/Moll taking the Acropolis and Sestrière rallies, Stirling Moss finishing second in the Tour de France, and Willy Mairesse winning the tough Liège-Rome-Liège contest in 1956 and again in 1957. There were other successes in American events but by now stiff opposition was being presented by the 250GT Ferrari coupé, and the 300SL Roadster had appeared (see following chapter).

Reverting to the journalists' findings about the 300SL coupé, after my brief flirtation with one at

Top *A close-up view of the side-grille on a 300SL*

Bottom *Nose details of the same car*

Top *For easy access to the driver's seat of a 300SL the stearing-wheel was made to hinge forward at its lower edge, as the picture shows, useful for the more portly German motorists!*

Bottom *Space for luggage in a 300SL was somewhat restricted but this did not prevent Daimler-Benz from offering these fitted suit-cases which straps retained behind the separate seats*

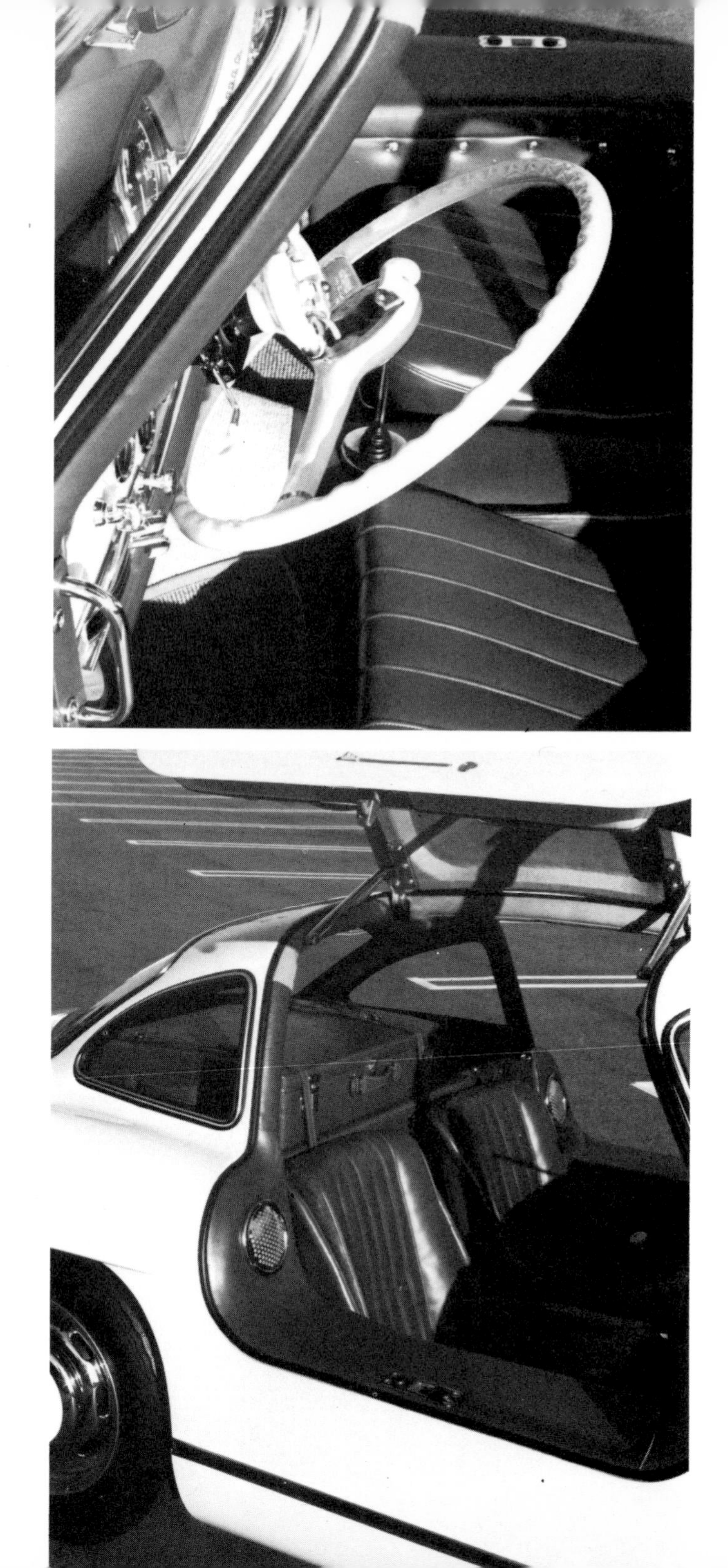

Silverstone I was able to make a pretty comprehensive assessment of a later, production model—registered RYT 28—early in 1956.

The experience was memorable for a number of things, apart from the impressive performance and sheer technical quality and complexity of the motor car itself.

In the first place, I planned to drive the press (or perhaps it doubled as a demonstration) 300SL down to Land's End from London and then rush it up to John O'Groats, with Michael Tee as co-driver and photographer. Now the 300SL with its drum brakes did not pull up from high speeds particularly well, and its swing-axle independent rear suspension rendered it difficult to drive quickly on twisty roads. However, we set off with the full optimism of youth (well, I was only 43 then!) but as I was driving actoss Bodmin Moor in Cornwall we were delayed by a nasty accident. The road narrowed at a bridge over a stream. To see if it was clear in this left-hand-drive car I had to pull to the right. Seeing a Ford Zehyr approaching I pulled back to my side and applied the brakes, stopping in plenty of time to give passage to this approaching car. Alas, its lady driver either thought I was coming through, or she lost the Ford while slowing for the narrow bridge. Anyway, she hit it, and the remote road from the West was blocked for a long time.

That decided us against continuing our run all the way to distant John O'Groats. However, Scotland was calling, so we settled for Fort William as our overnight stop. In Glasgow we paused to telephone an hotel, asking when they stopped serving dinner. They explained that being so far away we would never make the normal meal-time, but that they would reserve something for us to eat. After which, Michael Tee took over, and I shall always recall the great run he gave me over the winding roads in heavy rain, the moorland scenery

Ready for the road, this 300SL coupé has larger headlamps than the original cars, and substantial bumpers

eerie in the fading light. Our 'personal Mille Miglia' brought us to our destination so rapidly that when we entered the hotel and announced that dinner had been promised us, the manager said unfortunately not, as he was only able to serve some guests who had booked in from Glasgow and who—looking at his watch—would not be arriving for a considerable time. Outside, the exhaust system of the travel-stained 300SL was going 'ping-ping-ping' as it cooled, parked not far from the manager's Morris Eight. . . .

On that trip, in assessing the car, which for the British market was on Dunlop 6.50 × 15 Extra Super Sport tyres, we did a total of 1348 exhilarating miles, at 15.9 mpg of Esso Extra. It was, contrastingly, a pleasure to get out of the 300SL, partly because

Here is another classic view of a 300SL, with both doors open, as if for flight

those gull-wing doors were apt to cause claustrophobia, partly because it was a delight to look again at the shapely coupé and admire its beautifully-made mechanicals.

Another reason why this experience was memorable was that Denis Jenkinson, who a year earlier had been Stirling Moss' partner in the 300SLR Mercedes-Benz when they won the Mille Miglia, had asked to borrow the 300SL for a night's dice over his personal road-circuit, somewhere in darkest Hampshire/Wiltshire. I was driving home from London to Hampshire to lend the Mercedes to him when, going decidedly quickly, I ran up to a police road-block at Frimley, where there used to be a tricky railway-bridge. I was able more or less to stop as required, with those dubious drum brakes, but

A 300SL coupé seen in terrain very suitable to its performance, if the driver is capable of reacting quickly to swing-axle traits . . .

then came the problem of speaking to the policeman, who was waiting at the *near-side* window. The gull-wing doors of a 300SL were never all that amenable to being opened in a hurry—had not Mercedes-Benz themselves tried pull-out handles, press-buttons and press-in handles for them?—and after I had fumbled with the off-side door I decided I had better try to unlatch the other one—which, of course, rose and smote the unsuspecting officer under his chin. It was only a routine check, he was very nice about it, and even knew why I drove fast motor cars, and he made no comment about my crabbing retardation. . . . What I did not know was that, after I had handed over the car to Denis, he would go and wind it up in the opposite direction, slap into that same police trap. . . . I duly went to bed, rather jealous of Jenks and his mate on their nocturnal Grand Prix. I had to return the 300SL to Mercedes early the next day and had asked for it back at a specified hour. When it failed to arrive on time I grew somewhat cross. Eventually I heard it outside and was asked by DSJ to come out and look at it. 'I don't want to look at it,' I roared, 'I've seen it for some days and now I am late for getting it back to London.' The reason he wanted me to inspect the car was because he had had an 'incident' with it and one side was somewhat crumpled. At the time Mercedes-Benz (UK) Limited were experiencing some difficulty over obtaining reasonably-low insurance-rates for this very fast and expensive vehicle, and any accidents were like a red rag to the proverbial bull to them. Knowing

Sports-car equipped for a sporting occasion . . .

A view showing the quite uncomplicated dashboard of the 300SL coupé, its white-rimmed steering-wheel, and the knob of the long, cranked gear-lever, also the seats upholstered in plaid cloth

this, I made Jenks take the thing back and explain. Anger receeded when they realized he was the 'Mille Miglia Jenkinson', who had helped them to that important road-racing victory. . . .

I reported on this exciting and informative road test as follows.

'Most people will agree that the most fantastic motor car from the performance point of view which is available in the ordinary way is the Mercedes-Benz 300SL from Stuttgart. Produced a few years ago by the famous German firm as an essay in space-frame construction and to discover and subsequently demonstrate how the post-war 3-litre six-cylinder engine designed for the 300 and 300S Mercedes-Benz could be developed into a reliable fuel-injection, semi-competition power unit, the 300SL was successful in finishing first and second at Le Mans in 1952 and 1-2-3 at Berne, and winning the sports-car race (in open form) at Nürburg that year, besides being second in the Mille Miglia to a 4.1-litre Ferrari, after victory in the Carrera Pan-America race the previous year.

Recording a production target for the production 300SL at Stuttgart

'Since then this 300SL has been in prestige-production and over 1,000 have been sold, for this exceedingly eye-worthy, fast and, above all, accelerative coupé has proved a ready means of parting wealthy Americans from their dollars. *Motor Sport* has not been unaware of this fabulous car. In the issue for November, 1954, we published impressions of trying one at Silverstone. In the October issue last year our Continental Correspondent recounted his experiences of motoring to the Arctic Circle in a 300SL, and in August, 1955, R. R. C. Walker described his experiences as the first person to own one of these cars in England. We now have pleasure in presenting a full road-test report on this, the fastest of the production Mercedes-Benz models, with particular reference to motoring on British roads.

'To remark that wherever it stops the 300SL causes interest and astonishment, from comment by small boys on its 160-m.p.h. speedometer to admiration for its bonnet full of complex machinery, is to state the obvious. The lines of the car are handsome and well blended, and the "gull's wing" doors provide that touch of the futuristic in keeping with its character. In fact, this Mercedes-Benz provides comfortable accommodation for two persons and their holiday luggage, with a maximum speed of 145 to 160+ m.p.h. according to axle ratio, with acceleration "out of this world" and a fuel consumption of 80-octane petrol of at least 15 m.p.g. from an engine developing 190 b.h.p. and running safely up to 6,400 r.p.m.

'Access to the interior is through the ingenious doors, which swing up under the action of spring-struts on hinges at the centre of the roof, their pull-out handles being revealed by pressing in a knurled projection on the door. It is necessary to climb in and out over wide door sills, a construction made necessary by the shape of the space-frame tubing, which requires modest lady passengers to wear slacks, shorts or jeans! On the inside, similar pull-out handles release the doors, which swing up automatically, safety-catches being provided for locking them at high speed—the apparent disadvantage being that in the event of an accident unconscious occupants are virtually trapped and that should the driver somehow contrive to get the car onto its roof neither door can be opened—but those who motor fast or fly usually possess an outlook suitably fatalistic not to let such morbid considerations mar their pleasure! The seats of the 300SL are separate, tartan-upholstered, easily-adjustable buckets, one each side of the trans-

No gull-wing car has been as successful as the Mercedes-Benz 300SL. They managed to make a virtue out of necessity—what alternative was there using their spaceframe chassis?

Above *Shot in California in 1983 this early coupé is virtually as supplied. Note red leather upholstery and no check*

Right *Classic line which everyone loved and Jaguar, Ferrari and Aston Martin owners feared*

Left *Understated dashboard with steering wheel in position. The interior followed Daimler-Benz tradition*

Below *Both cream and silver grey are common colours for the coupés. Unlike the cream car this one does not have overriders and although British registered still has left hand drive*

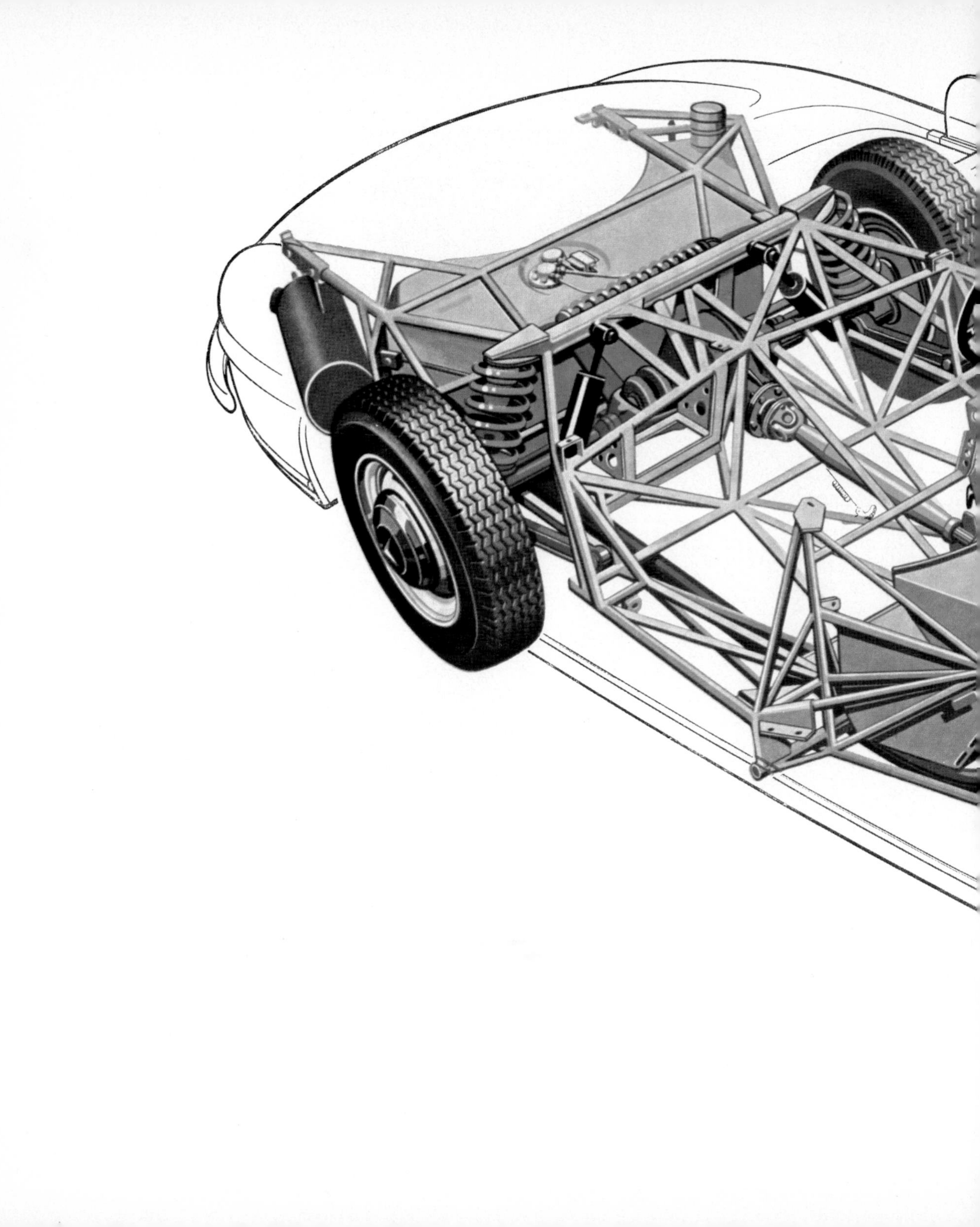

Taken from the 300SL brochure dated 11/60 this superb colour 'see-through' drawing clarifies the chassis technology of the Roadster

NNG 607V

Top *Two seater Roadster with large boot lid and hidden-away rag top. Highly coveted classic Mercedes the like of which will never be seen again in production*

Above *Red contrasting hub cap centres and yet another headlamp style (with headlamp reflecters of foreign origin?) complete this trio of Roadsters*

Left *Magnificent red Roadster with hardtop and knock-off wire spoke wheels. Note all-in-one headlamp glasses*

Fairly sad looking Roadster for sale at Hershey in October 1982. With a refurbished hood and a repaint, but still in black, this could be a beautiful specimen in no time

mission tunnel; they are hard, a little short in the squab, yet generally very comfortable, more particularly as they hold the occupants securely throughout the "g"-loadings imposed by the car's immense performance. There is good leg room, sitting high with one's feet in wells in the floor.

The dash layout is somewhat "American" in its employment of plating and lots of shining, unlabelled knobs, but these minor controls are of good quality. Spaced right across the plated strip at the base of the dash, from left to right of this left-hand-drive car, are a pair of sliding controls to regulate air supply to left of the windscreen and driver's legs, choke, parking-lights switch, dash-lamp switch, lamps switch (which has four positions: all off, electrics, including "blinkers," other than lamps, side and tail-lamps, head-lamps), Bomora ignition key, which when turned operates the starter, two-speed wiper switch for the self-parking wipers, sliding controls for heater, passenger's horn-button, cigar-lighter, switch to operate heater fan for use in heating or ventilating the car when it is stationary, and sliding controls for passenger's screen and leg-temperature control. Additional controls are the ignition advance and retard (not normally used by the driver), reserve fuel pump switch, which also acts as a means of starting the engine if it is reluctant when hot, together with warning lights for choke-out, "blinkers" in use, headlamps full-beam and dynamo charge. The passenger is reminded of the potentialities of the ride by a "300SL" motif in front of him or her, and beside this is an accurate Vdo clock. Immediately before the driver in a hooded upsweep of the dash are the Vdo 4-in. speedometer (reading to 160 m.p.h., with trip and total milometers) and rev.-counter, the latter recording up to 7,000 r.p.m. Both these instruments have steady, clear white needles which move round the dials in the same plane. There are four small Vdo

Travel-stained—the 300SL road-tested by Motor Sport

instruments for fuel contents (gauge calibrated R, ½, F), oil pressure, which varies very considerably with engine speed, oil temperature and water temperature. Normally, oil temperature is about 140 deg. F. and water temperature 175 deg. F. The oil pressure at high r.p.m. is 70/75 lb. sq. in.

The 16½-in. two-spoke steering wheel hinges under for easy access to and exit from the driving seat by pulling a plunger under the boss. In its hub, proudly displaying the Mercedes-Benz three-pointed star, is the push-button for the reasonably-penetrating horn. Vertical grab-handles are placed at each end of the dash and there is a covered ashtray (for smokers of Havanna cigars?) before the passenger on the off side of the deep dash sill. Further handles enable the doors to be pulled down

Photographed somewhere between Land's End and Scotland during a fast-driven road-test of RYT 28 for Motor Sport *in 1956, during which nearly 1400 miles were covered at 15.9 mpg of petrol*

easily after you have entered. The central mirror has a flick control to obviate dazzle but, mounted on the dash sill, provides a poor view and would probably be better hung from the roof—maybe the excuse is that nothing follows a 300SL for long!

'Sitting at the wheel of a 300SL you find yourself well to the left, with a great expanse of motor car to the off side, the more embarrassing because the body is appreciably wider than the track, being, indeed, 5 ft. 10½ in. There is excellent forward visibility over the long but low bonnet with its two "power-bulges," that on the near side to clear the valve cover, but the screen pillars are rather thick. The pedals are close spaced, so that it is possible to "heel-and-toe" when changing gear while braking. The hand-brake, which has an adjacent adjuster, is

Top *Trueing-up the spaceframe of a 300SL*

Bottom *The 300SL assembly-line at Sindelfingen, with the complicated spaceframe of a 300SL in the foreground and engines awaiting installation on the left*

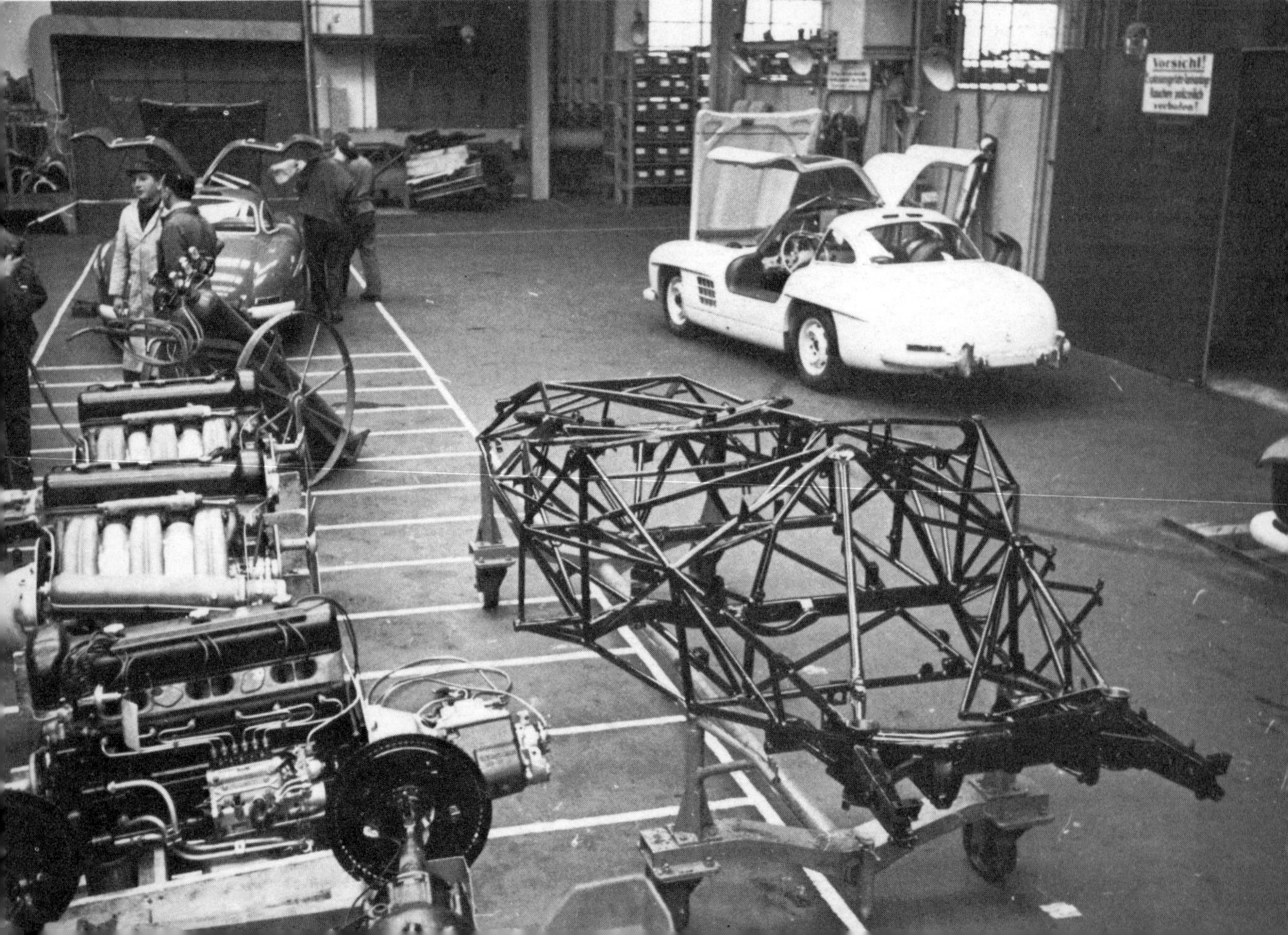

for parking only, being far forward on the left. The rigid remote-control central gear-lever is rather far back for the right hand; the gear positions are marked on the knob and reverse is well over to the left of the forward gear locations, which are conventional, except that this is a left-hand-drive vehicle, so that top and third are off-side. The lever is not spring-loaded.

'Under the dash, from left to right, are the tommy-handle for releasing the bonnet and the screen-squirt knob. The interior lamp is above the screen, between the sun-vizors. Another tommy-handle under the dash opens a scuttle ventilator. At night, with the dash lamp off, all dials save that of the clock remain faintly and very effectively visible. The only warning light which dazzles is that of the "blinkers" reminder.

'Luggage accommodation consists of a platform behind the seats which will comfortably accommodate a couple of large suitcases and many smaller objects. The lockable boot lid lifts, and is secured by a prop, to reveal the fuel tank and filler, spare wheel, and tools, but coats can be packed in round the wheel. Some water entered the boot in heavy rain. At the rear of the roof are two open ventilator ducts, so placed aerodynamically that no water or draughts appeared able to enter, and the car never, under any conditions, misted-up screen, side or rear windows. Couple this with a heating and ventilating system the equal in efficiency and adjustment to that of a luxury air-liner, augmented by opening panels, with effective catches, in the side windows—moreover, for summer motoring the whole glass panel of the window is detachable by pulling out a peg—and it will be evident that after lowering yourself into this impressive Mercedes-Benz and locking yourself in, you are certain of comfort. The body is commendably silent and the ingenious doors proved rain-proof in a tropical

Top *The 300SL laid bare. The complex chassis of small-bore tubes can be studied and it is apparent why this model could only be had in left-hand-drive form*

Bottom *Exclusive assembly-line. The 300SLs being built up on the left trolley-track and being given their bodies on the reverse track*

deluge, save for a little seepage onto one door sill, which didn't reach the occupants, and water which reached the driver's seat *via* the heating ducts. Considerable draught entered round the hand-brake, however, and towards the end of the test the steering column started to squeak. Other sounds were the ventilator fan as it was rotated by the air-stream and the loud click of the reserve fuel pump. The driver's door-catch tended to jam, having "picked-up" in its socket. After the car has been running at low speeds in traffic considerable petrol vapour is smelt and the engine "fluffs" until it is cleared by faster driving.

In lieu of disc brakes, Mercedes-Benz at first used drum brakes for the 300SL but of wide formation and deeply turbo-finned, as shown in this factory assembly picture

'The alligator bonnet hinges at the front, being held upen by a strut, to reveal the mysteries of the fuel-injection engine and its equally-mysterious auxiliaries. The engine is inclined to the near side to secure a low bonnet line and the width of the valve cover is impressive, and reminiscent of commercial-vehicle practice. The dip-stick is combined with the oil filler for the dry-sump oil tank and, like the coolant filler for the remote header-tank, is readily accessible.

'You are now acquainted with the creature-comforts of the 300SL and require a brief introduction to its technicalities.

'The chassis is a multi-tube, longitudinally-stressed, space-frame with the lightweight Sindelfingen body in unit with it. The weight of this structure is quoted as 2,556 lb. Front suspension is by wish-bones and coil-springs, rear independent suspension by coil-springs and swing axles. The 10.23-in. 2LS hydraulic brakes are vacuum-servo assisted and have wide steel drums with alloy turbo-fin coolers. The 3-litre, 88 by 85-mm., 2,996-c.c. engine has a Bosch PES 6KL 70/320 R2 fuel-injection pump and Bosch coil ignition. The overhead valves are actuated by an o.h. camshaft driven by a twin roller chain. A dry-sump lubrication system, with oil cooler, is employed, the oil tank on the near side of the engine having a capacity of 4 gallons. Pressurized pump cooling is used, with a belt-driven four-bladed fan, the total coolant capacity being 4.1 gallons, and a thermostat being incorporated. The balanced crankshaft runs in seven plain bearings. The Bosch injection pump and injectors are not visible from above, being on the near side of the cylinder block, but very imposing is the big air-intake manifold on the off side. The Bosch distributor is at the front of the engine on the near side, supplying the Bosch W280T2 plugs on the same side. The engine develops

Overalled operatives devote much care to the assembly of the 300SL chassis, with the back axle being given its shockabsorbers, in the foreground

240 b.h.p. at the clutch when not driving such auxiliaries as the dynamo, etc., but the more normally quoted output is 190 b.h.p. at 6,400 r.p.m., with 6,000 r.p.m. safe for continuous use; for example in the indirect gears. The compression-ratio is 8.55 to 1. The gearbox has synchromesh of the baulk-ring type on all gears, and axle ratios of 3.42 to 1 and 3.25 to 1 are available on request in addition to the standard ratio of 3.64 to 1, as on the car we had for test. Tyres are 6.50 by 15 and either sports or racing types are fitted. Fuel feed from the 28-gallon fuel tank is by a Bosch FP/KLA22 K1 pump, and the fuel-injector operates at a pressure of 568–682 lb./sq. in. The exhaust system is on the off side, twin clusters merging into a $2\frac{5}{8}$-in. tail-pipe.

'The air intake at the front of the car incorporates the three-pointed star and the name "Mercedes-Benz" appears on the body on the driver's side only.

The wheelbase is 7 ft. 10½ in., ground clearance approximately 5 in., and the turning circle approximately 37¾ ft. The car comes with an excellent instruction book and some intriguing tools, including a gauge and supply of weights for wheel-balancing.

'You have now become familiar with this Mercedes-Benz in the garage and are free to take it out on the road. Even before an opportunity arises to open it up it impresses as a real motor car—decidedly! In second there is a loud, rather rough, gear-noise, which increases to a musical howl in third, which can be held, incidentally, to nearly 100 m.p.h., after changing up at around 70. Engine speed goes up instantly and cleanly as the throttle is opened, sending the needle of the rev.-counter surging round the dial. The acceleration is "out of this world," for apart from the power developed, the power curve is such that the thrust goes on building up without a break, so that even from 100 m.p.h. onwards there is this sense of being hurled forward, the exhaust note remaining constant, until at 5,500 r.p.m. in third gear the noise of gears, engine and exhaust is that of a true competition car. Mere figures cannot convey the vivid, continued acceleration of the 300SL, which enables 90/100 m.p.h. to be reached almost everywhere and 110/125 m.p.h. to come up along short straights. Twice we reached 5,700 r.p.m. in top gear, equal to 126½ m.p.h. with the standard back-axle ratio, once near Salisbury and once on an open road in Scotland. On an arterial road near London, 6,100 r.p.m., or over 135 m.p.h., was recorded. The maximum depends purely on traffic conditions and the driver's disposition, up to an absolute of about 146 m.p.h. In terms of figures, this Mercedes-Benz achieves 0–50 m.p.h. in 5.7 sec., 0–70 m.p.h. in 8.5 sec., and 0–100 m.p.h. or a s.s. ¼-mile in a shade over 16 sec. Even more impressive is its ability to increase speed from 50 to 70 m.p.h. in second gear in a mere 4 sec., or to go from 60 to 80 m.p.h. in third gear in a matter of 5.1 sec., after which 100 m.p.h. is reached, in top gear, after less than 8 sec. have elapsed, and even from "the ton" a velocity of two-miles-a-minute can be achieved after another 9 sec. have gone by.

'Yet the acceleration, accompanied by a healthy power-roar from under the broad bonnet, is even more impressive than the sheer speed of the car. Rob Walker aptly compared driving a fast car on English roads with making huffs at draughts, and in a 300SL you have the best means possible of "huffing" in safety. The sense of being propelled forward with undiminished acceleration up to two-miles-a-minute if necessary, by the unleased smooth power of an engine which feels completely reliable, is not only an exhilarating sensation for the occupants, and one which makes passing other vehicles a very fleeting, and therefore safe, operation—it looks exceptionally impressive to those you pass!

'At speed the wind noise is very low, unless the ventilator windows are open, while it is possible to converse comfortably when cruising at 100 m.p.h.

'The steering is accurate but heavy towards lock, pulling against the castor action, although the latter is not self-centring. There is an element not of lost-motion, for there is none, but rather of sponginess at very low speeds, but in action the steering becomes lighter and, geared $2\frac{1}{3}$ turns lock-to-lock, enables the car to be placed accurately. It is rather "dead" steering, hardly any road-wheel motion being transmitted, and no column vibration. The weight distribution is such that this Mercedes-Benz needs concentration to keep it straight, for it tends to wander, and once it departs from the intended course it asks some time before the driver can coax it back. The brakes, while stopping this 24-cwt. car very reasonably from three-figure speeds, especially

Great moment. The coupé bodyshell is at last mated with its chassis, after all the care and devotion given to both in the Daimler-Benz factories, by skilled operatives under great engineers

if aided by changing down, as the handbook recommends, are rather slow, then fierce, in action, as the servo takes effect, and consequently to apply them hard on a slippery surface is a practice to be avoided whenever possible. Too hard an application of the brakes produces a smell of hot lining within the car and tends to cause snaking. The brakes also squeaked slightly at times.

The suspension is quite soft, enabling the car to be driven fast over bad surfaces, but there is a slight penalty to pay in respect of some roll when cornering and over undulations the action of the swing-axle rear suspension could be discerned.

A work of art. The power unit of the Mercedes-Benz 300SL, showing, among other items, the Bosch fuel-injection pump and the lubrication arrangements

'The clutch is light and showed no desire to slip, and the gear change is pleasant but requires decisive (and therefore not lightning-quick) movements, too hurried a cog-swap without correct synchronisation of crankshaft and layshaft speed resulting in an audible "clonk."

'The exhaust note is never objectionable and the 300SL can be driven unobtrusively through towns, only the music of the lower gears revealing to the occupants the car's impatience for clear roads.

'Naturally, with nearly 200 true horse-power available it is necessary to open up with discretion on slippery surfaces, after which that shattering pick-up comes in to propel you relentlessly forward to whatever cruising speed is appropriate.

'Power-sliding corners is one of the joys a skilled driver can indulge in with this car, and it is significant that between Glasgow and Fort William, in pouring rain, a gale, and at night, we averaged 54 m.p.h. for an hour's driving on roads so twisting that top gear was seldom if ever engaged, thirty miles being covered in half-an-hour of similar motoring.

'Previous to this we had driven from Basingstoke to Land's End at an average speed of better than 56 m.p.h., in spite of much lorry traffic, roads covered in places with melting snow, and a six-minute stop for petrol. The best hour's run accounted for 63 miles and obviously, on clearer occasions, particularly late at night, the 300SL would prove capable of 70-m.p.h. averages in safety on narrow British roads. Yet should Auntie borrow it, she can drive along at 700 r.p.m. in a top gear which gives 22.2 m.p.h. per 1,000 r.p.m. without anxiety on the machinery's part, acceleration, thanks no doubt to fuel injection, being clean as soon as the accelerator is depressed. No doubt, however, she, as we were, would be awed by the width of the car—it is necessary to remember this when taking roundabouts or meeting other vehicles, for the body is appreciably wider than the track and with left-hand drive this is sometimes a little disturbing.

'The 7½-in. inbuilt Bosch headlamps are adequate for using the available performance at night; they have a foot dipper.

'Apart from the aforementioned "fluffing" and the smell of petrol after prolonged slow running, the Mercedes-Benz 300SL functioned with entire reliability while it was in our hands, which was for a matter of 1,348 miles. In this distance five pints of oil were required and the consumption of Esso Extra, in very fast driving, worked out at 15.9 m.p.g. The engine always commenced impeccably with momentary use of the choke, and didn't prove temperamental when hot. The fuel reserve of approximately two gallons is useful and although no warning light is provided the noise of the reserve pump working is sufficient reminder. Apart from the few items listed earlier the only faults were occasional reluctance of the screen wipers to self-park at the first movement of the switch, and momentary blockage of a squirt, which cured itself. The Dunlop tyres proved silent on corners, held their pressure and the racing-pattern treads showed no wear. Incidentally, conditions during the test included dry, wet and snow-ridged roads, torrential rain, mist and gale-force winds, not to mention scores of miles of heavy traffic.

'Although no cubby-hole or door pockets are provided, the wide door sills and transmission tunnel provide useful stowage, and so stable is the car that small objects "stay put" in these places reasonably well, although when driven really fast this car is one of the few which, in spite of its comfortable ride, can tire a passenger by the sudden backwards, forwards and sideways movements imposed.

'It is truly difficult to convey on paper the fascination, amounting almost to awe, that this car imposes on those who drive it or are driven in it. It is the modern and logical equivalent of the 36/220 and 38/250 models of the past and therefore is a typical Mercedes-Benz. It is not for Auntie because, although she could drive it slowly without harming it, that would be such a shocking waste. It is not for portly business men with fat stomachs full of good food and wine topped by a layer of beer. It is for experienced drivers who like to motor at speeds upwards of 90 m.p.h. whenever possible. There are some experiences money cannot buy but you can have a Mercedes-Benz 300SL for £4,651. . . .'

I was naturally by no means the only journalist to be impressed by the Mercedes-Benz 300SL. One of the first from England was Gordon Wilkins, who was permitted to try one of the actual Le Mans cars

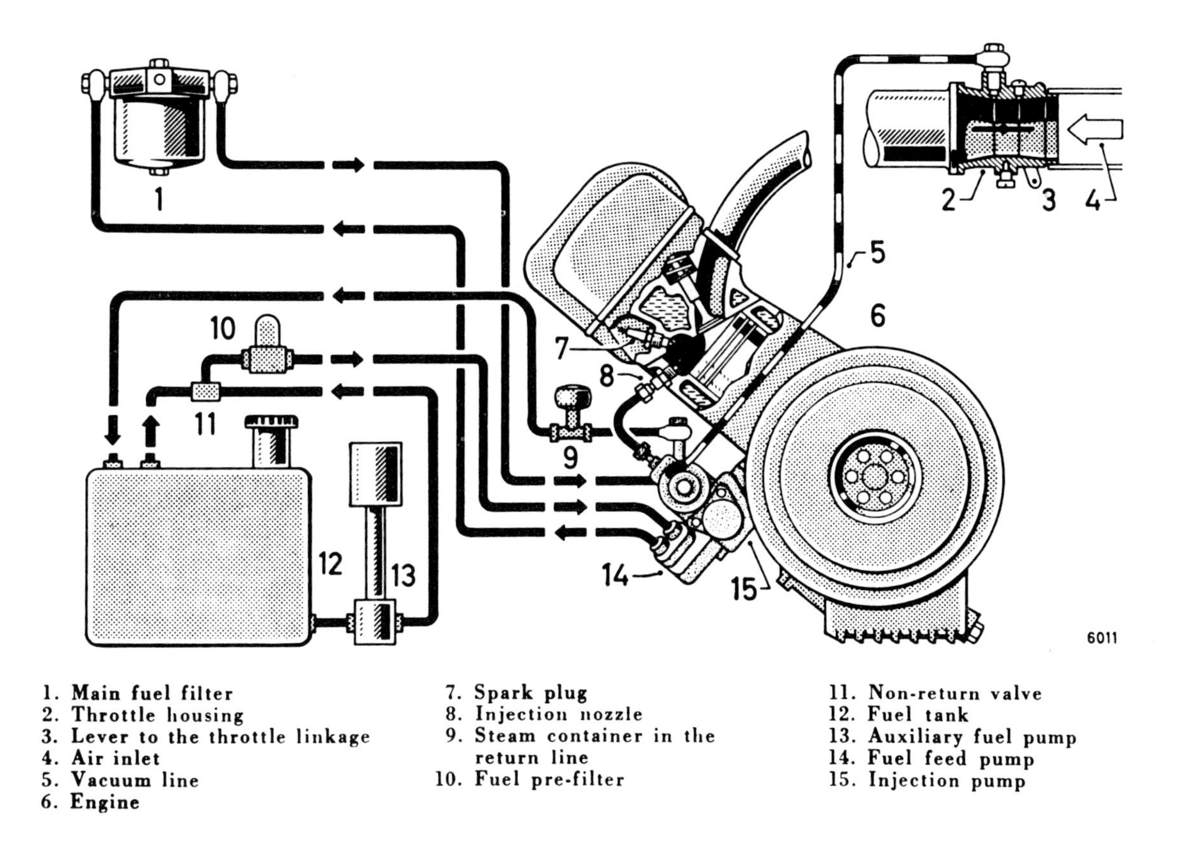

Fuel-system diagram for the 300SL engine

two hours after that race had finished, in 1952, taking his wife as his passenger. This was, of course, a factory competition car, not a production model, but it is interesting that Wilkins reckoned he did 0 to 100 mph in 18.2 sec without setting the road on fire. Although he remarked on the noise in the cockpit, which had apparently caused Klenk to use a small microphone in order to converse with Kling during the race, and about the hard ride on shock absorbers set for racing, he obviously appreciated the great potential of the car as a road-going proposition. Incidentally, the tachometer of that 1952 Le Mans coupé was red-lined at 6300 rpm, and it was said that the drivers were using only about

6100 rpm, equivalent to approximately 152 mph on the 3.25:1 axle ratio. Wilkins was cautious in his comments about the brakes—they 'were good but not specially powerful at high speeds', although a car he had tried earlier, in Stuttgart, which had been specially equipped with a vacuum-servo for Caracciola, was found to be better. By the way, that 0–100 mph in about 18.2 sec compares with the time of rather more than 16 sec for the later catalogue-model I drove in 1956, using an axle ratio of 3.64:1 and 15 in. wheels.

Among those who tried the car in this country in 1954, at the aforesaid pre-view, was S. C. H. 'Sammy' Davis, who had extensive knowledge of the make. He recalled, in fact, his first contact with a Mercedes 51 years earlier, but criticized the 300SL, as then constituted, for having a fuel pump that had to be switched on to start the engine when it was warm and for sparking plugs that were out of sight and hard to get at, due to the inclined power-unit. He also expressed the view that such a car should not be available to the inexperienced for ordinary road use (those high insurance rates!) but 'was really thrilled by the machine, . . . for it has the power of intoxication which comes from perfection of performance well above 100 mph. After the experience of that it is hard to come down to human level because one has ridden with the gods'. I felt much the same, as I drove away from Silverstone that day in 1954

The 300SL which John Bolster had hoped to report on for *Autosport* was returned to Germany before he could do so, but in January 1955 he was able to conduct his test. He quoted the car as a 140 mph 3-litre of beauty and superb performance. To get a mean timed-speed of 140.6 mph he took the engine to 6250 rpm in top, as the test car had the lowest of the three available axle-ratios. His 0–100 mph time was 16.2 sec and he got 15 mpg. *The*

Another scene from the Mercedes-Benz assembly line, with a 300SL power unit being lowered into the space frame chassis

Autocar confirmed all this in March that year, after testing PLB 23. Its speed findings were 44, 70, 98 and 135 mph in the gears, the mean timed maximum being 128½ mph; 0–60 mph took 8.8 sec, 0–100 mph a matter of 21.0 sec, the Mercedes going over the standing start ¼-mile in 16.1 sec. Note how this all compares favourably with a high-performance car made today. Fuel consumption averaged 18.4 mpg over *The Autocar*'s 746-mile stint. But it, too, noted that the swing-axle rear suspension had to be treated with respect, though the brakes, even when used for rapidly descending Shap Fell, were entirely satisfactory.

That 1955 car can be regarded as the normal catalogued version of a 300SL. It was then priced at £4392 15*s* 10*d* (with purchase tax) in Great Britain.

Other writers saw the 300SL in other lights. The technical editor of *Motoring Life*, having over-estimated the engine size by a litre, wrote of a maximum of 165 mph after reaching 150 mph on the road, and 0–100 mph in 21 sec, with 100 mph in 3rd gear, all at 20 mpg, but Maurice Smith, of *The Autocar*, spoke of a 'big push in the back' and acceleration from 20 to 120 mph in top gear. He did however remark that although when in the air he used to adjust bank and rudder to avoid slip or skid, he was not entirely happy about having to corner with power on in the Mercedes. On a run to Cheltenham and back to London he thought the clutch heavy, and the gear change laborious, but he had only praise for the servo brakes, which were almost up to Rolls-Royce mechanical-servo standards. 'It is polite to either love or hate your friends,' concluded Maurice, 'indifference is an insult.' His criticisms of the 300SL were, he said, made in that spirit.

By now testers were getting accustomed to the steering wheel you hinged flat for easier access, and the window glasses that you had to remove for full ventilation because such radically-curved glass could not be wound-down or slid-open. . . . It would seem that your view of the car's performance depended on which motor journal you read. *Sports Car Illustrated* quoted 139½ mph (137.8 mph, mean) and 0 to 100 mph in 17.7 sec, or 14.0 sec from the tuned version, in 1956, but Denis Jenkinson, who had already experienced the 300SLR in the Mille Miglia victory with Moss, preferred something more objective, going to the Arctic Circle in a 300SL coupé, for a holiday with Count von Trips, in the car that its owner, Eric Lundgren, had just been racing at Karskoga, for *his* report in *Motor Sport*.

By this time the 300SL was in limited but steady production with construction being divided between Stuttgart and Sindelfingen. If the 300SL was not exactly a hand-built car in the Rolls-Royce sense, it was a low-volume production to which the meticulous standards of Daimler-Benz were given special emphasis. Inspectors checked assembly very carefully indeed, paying attention to such items as the fit of the gull-wing doors and body joints. Foreign journalists going to the plant would be shown round by Prince von Urach, who was so well-fitted to look after the world's pressmen. They could not fail to be impressed.

By 1954/55 production of 300SLs was at the rate of 50 a month. One of the first private owners in England was that well-known motor-racing personality and enthusiast, Rob Walker, who took delivery of his coupé, ROB 2, on 31 December 1954.

A week later another had been delivered to David Brown. By the way, although the silver finish of the bodywork was standard, other colours were available to special order, and a black gull-wing coupé looked particularly elegant. Reverting to Rob Walker's opinions about his new Mercedes-Benz,

Body dimensional drawings of the 300SL gull-wing coupé found in the British handbook

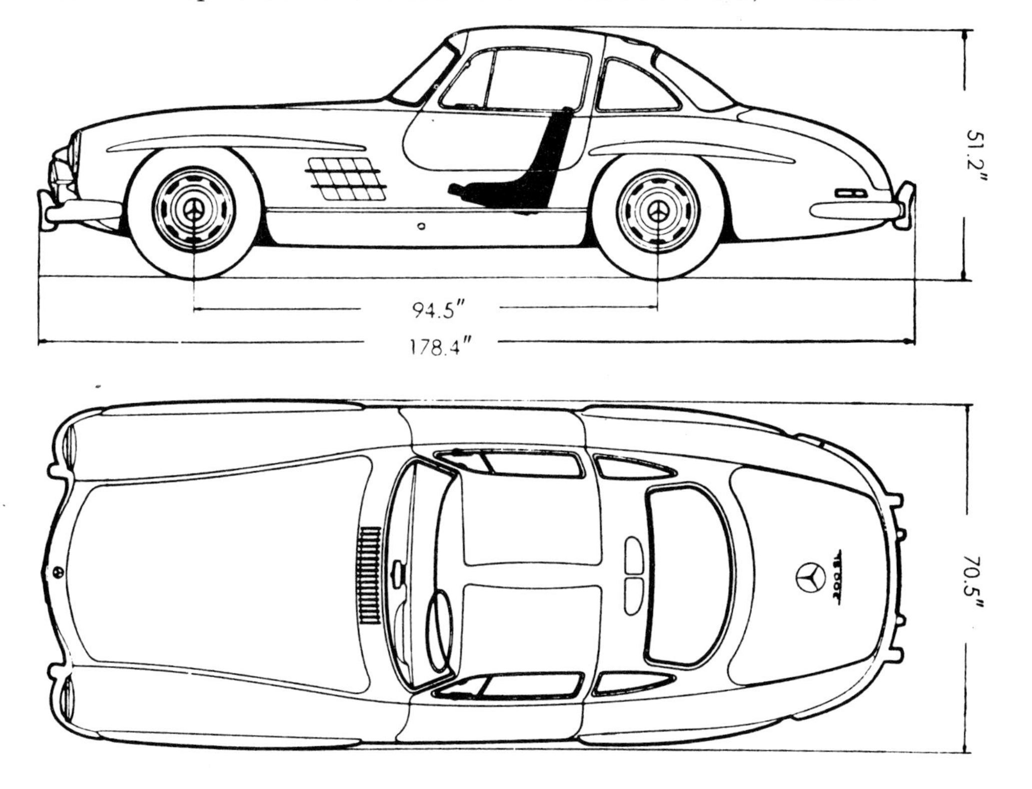

which he expressed in the very amusing and readable article I persuaded him to write for *Motor Sport* in 1955, I remember he said he didn't find that its left-hand steering was too much of a disadvantage 'because the average Englishman drives in the middle of the road and it is easier to see around his left side than his right'! The servo brakes Walker found rather too sudden in an emergency, it being possible to lock up all four drums at 90 mph, expressing the view, as an aside, that he could never understand why Mercedes-Benz spent all that time fooling about with air brakes when they could have been experimenting with disc brakes. As for the speed of ROB 2, Walker noted that various authorities had quoted maximum-speed figures for the 300SL coupé which had varied slightly. His own car, on the low axle-ratio, was capable of 0 to 60 mph in 7.2 sec, 0 to 100 mph in 16.2 sec, 0 to 120 mph in 25.8 sec, with a top speed of 140.5 mph under good conditions. Driving in the Gosport speed trials Rob Walker covered the standing-start ¼-mile in 15.7 sec and the s.s. kilometre in 30.8 sec, under very wet conditions. On the road his speedometer would show 150 mph for a true speed of 135 mph, and this optimism of that instrument was a cause for regret.

Rob Walker thought at first that the handling on corners was difficult, rather like driving on ice, but after Stirling Moss had assured him it was very good after one had got used to the swing-axle rear-end, Rob thought no more about it, and attributed his initial worry to having come straight off an Aston Martin DB2. As for reliability, the works said they did not want to see the car again for 20,000 miles, apart from routine servicing, when the engine would require decarbonizing; the thin SAE 10 oil apparently helping in this respect. The only trouble with ROB 2 in the first 8000 miles was that a windscreen-wiper arm fell off. . . . It was nice that, although few 300SLs had been sold to English-speaking people by 1954, all the under-bonnet instructions were—*in English!* Rob Walker ran his Mercedes-Benz in a few competitions, winning his class at a West Essex CC speed trial. That brought a letter of congratulations from Stuttgart, to which 'Lofty' England of Jaguar's replied that had Rob been driving an XK140 he would have received a *telegram.* . . ! What very much impressed the experienced Mr. Walker about 300SL motoring was the smoothness and silence of the beast—from 15 mph in top gear without jerk or judder, to 130 mph when there was room, talking to your right-hand man (or woman) without raising your voice; of wind-noise there was none. Mrs. Walker drove ROB 2, taking Mike Hawthorn round Ibsley in it, and the Duke of Richmond and Gordon, Tom Rolt, Jack Fairman, Rodney Clarke and Gilbert Harding all had rides in it with Rob.

Chapter 4
Later developments

The 300SL in the forms in which it first appeared was exciting by any standards and it possessed a 'character' very definitely all its own. But Mercedes-Benz did not rest on these laurels. The next move, after the original 300SL coupé had been satisfactorily put on the market for the delection of keen and experienced motoring enthusiasts all over the world, was the development of an even higher-performance coupé and the preparation of an open version—the 300SL Roadster. Work was also put in hand to overcome the objections some drivers had to the uncertainties of high-speed cornering with the swing-axle rear-suspension, which could promote excessive oversteer. Tests were also conducted, by the Daimler-Benz factory and by private owners, to ascertain the true top speed of the coupé 300SL.

In May 1955 a 300SL was taken to the *Autobahn* just North of Munich, the car used for these official maximum speed tests being the one which John Fitch had used for the Mille Miglia. It had been checked over thoroughly, of course, after the race. The car had been given a special axle-ratio of 3.09:1, probably a thought optimistically high, and driver Mische, of the Racing and Development Department, extended it to around 5700 rpm in top gear.

The sports-coupé we all craved, back in the 1950s!

The result was an average, two-way speed over a flying-start kilometre of $155\frac{1}{2}$ mph. So the good aerodynamics of the body-shape were confirmed, for the engine had never boasted of exceptional horse-power outputs, these ranging from 49 bhp per litre at 5550 rpm on a cr of 6.7:1, 66 bhp per litre at 5800 rpm on a cr of 8.3:1 and 68 bhp per litre at the same rpm, on a cr of 12.1:1.

To show that this 300SL was no freak, with its high top gear, two well-known motoring writers, Gordon Wilkins and Wilson McComb, then drove it from Munich to Frankfurt that day and were able to average 78.6 mph for the journey, thus proving this 155 mph motor car to be a practical, if a formidable, road machine.

Why the luggage mostly went inside the 300SL coupé. There was more room in the Roadster's boot. Note the big fuel filler cap beneath the boot-lid, and the twin exhaust-pipes

That such a maximum speed from a 300SL was not exactly a freak performance was indicated when American private owners had their Mercedes timed at Bonneville Salt Flats, during the SCTA's National Speed Trials, one car being timed to achieve fractionally more than 152 mph over the out-and-back run, while other stock examples managed speeds of 143$\frac{3}{4}$ and 148.2 mph along the years.

The normal 300SL body was constructed of steel for its main panels, and light-alloy panelling for the bonnet-lid, rear decking and doors. Such construction was used in most of the coupés supplied to

The light bonnet-lid of a 300SL lifted from the front, to reveal the imposing induction-tract of the fuel-injection engine. Note how far over the cambox cover lies

private owners. The total production of such Mercedes-Benz was 1371 cars. But a rather more exciting edition of the traditional gull-wing coupé was to follow, in which the entire body was made of aluminium panelling. This saved 176 lb, and gave a dry weight of 2381 lb. These special lightweight 300SLs were supplied for racing by special customers, or for fast road driving.

A special camshaft was also available, replacing the normal camshaft which was the same as the one used in the Mercedes-Benz 300 saloon. This 'sports-cam' gave a different valve timing and increased the lift of the exhaust valves by a matter of 0.6 mm. The timing alteration meant that the inlet valves, with tappets correctly set, opened 2 degrees earlier and closed 2 degrees later, and that the exhaust valves opened 19 degrees earlier and closed 7 degrees later. It was also possible to have centre-lock Rudge-type wire wheels for your 300SL coupé, instead of the bolt-on wheels, equipped with nave-plates, of the normal model. Incidentally, these cars, in whatever condition of tune, were essentially two-seaters, and as the space behind the seats was restricted, Mercedes-Benz made available a pair of special suitcases, intended to fit into the space above the rear shelf, and retained by two straps. However as these cases were somewhat large, it was no easier to load or unload one's luggage than it was to get into or out of this low coupé with any attempt at grace.

In England Rob Walker was one of the first customers to take delivery of a lightweight 300SL

Rob Walker's famous 300SL—SLR 1—photographed at a club gathering

Used for the tour to the Arctic Circle by von Trips and Denis Jenkinson, this 300SL is clean and neat at this juncture

gull-wing coupé, as he had been of the ordinary model with the softer camshaft. His car also had harder springs and stiffer shock absorbers than standard. He flew to Stuttgart in 1956, at a time when only the first two of these 'hotter' cars had been built. The price asked for them had not increased, although Rob was of the opinion that this probably implied that they were sold at a loss to the Daimler-Benz company. The other 'lightweight' had been offered to another great enthusiast for fine motor cars, Jack Atkins, who, like Rob, already owned one of the early 300SLs and knew the delights of such motoring—indeed, he intended to keep his first one and possess two of them!

Amateur participation with 300SL gull-wings in the Swedish Grand Prix of 1955

The trip to collect these respective lightweight 300SLs, as Rob Walker described in *Motor Sport* at the time, was quite an occasion. Jack Atkins took with him, when they left from Heathrow, Owen Williams, of Woking Motors, the well-known Mercedes-Benz distributors, and Rob was accompanied by the manager of his motor racing department, Stan Jolliffe, who was then the secretary of the British Racing Mechanics' Club. They flew *via* Zurich in a Vickers Viscount, on which one of the flaps stuck down and had to be retrieved by hand-winding, which must have been disturbing for Rob Walker, as he had been a RNAS-pilot during the war. On arrival at Stuttgart airport the party was greeted by Herr Rapp, the Daimler-Benz export manager, who took them in his Mercedes-Benz 180D saloon to the dispersal point for new cars. Only after they had checked to see that all the equipment of both cars was in order were they permitted to drive them away, to an hotel in Stuttgart at which rooms had been reserved by Daimler-Benz. Next day they interviewed Uhlenhaut (who was born in England and, as I am aware, speaks excellent English) about any points concerning 300SLs which might be troubling them. Rob wondered about tyres, his new coupé being fitted, he had noticed, with Continentals. The answer was that after high-speed tests by Mercedes these tyres were made to their exact requirements—so the new owner of a 'lightweight' was satisfied, and was to find this equipment entirely to his liking.

Herrmann and Eger on the starting-ramp before the 1955 Mille Miglia, with one of four 300SLRs. They retired with petrol leak problems

In America and Canada the 300SL was used for competition work by amateur racing men, as here, with a coupé dodging a spinning Austin-Healey at Harewood in 1956

Rob then bravely raised the then-pertinent question of why, even for racing, Mercedes-Benz continued to use drum instead of disc brakes. Uhlenhaut replied that this was because Germany was not as far advanced in disc brake techniques and construction as we were in Britain, and that on some kinds of corners, on those used for the Swiss Grand Prix, for instance, an air-brake would slow a car effectively when a disc brake, reluctant to back-off, might not. They then enquired about whether or

not they could purchase a 300SLR (see Chapter 5), but the answer was a polite but emphatic 'No'—with sensible reasons for the refusal. . . .

Anyway, Rob Walker was very satisfied with his lightweight 300SL. After these British customers had been lunched in the senior executives' dining room by Herr Wilhelm, one of the Daimler-Benz directors, they followed Herr Rapp for some ten miles to the *Autobahn* and set off in their prized new possessions. The running-in speeds had been set at

Certain types of European rallying readily suited the 300SL. This mountain hairpin shows its handling traits

Overleaf *The gull-wing coupé was followed by the more practical 300SL Roadster, a model in production from 1957 to 1962, seen here in production guise*

Top *The folded hood fits into the boot-space of the Roadster*

Top right *The entire Roadster body was lowered onto the 300SL chassis frame from an overhead runway*

Bottom right *Meahanics work in comfort, preparing the Roadster bodyshells for final flatting and painting*

Bottom *Visitors to a motor show admire the Roadster with its hood or top up. It seems that the paying public have yet to be granted admission*

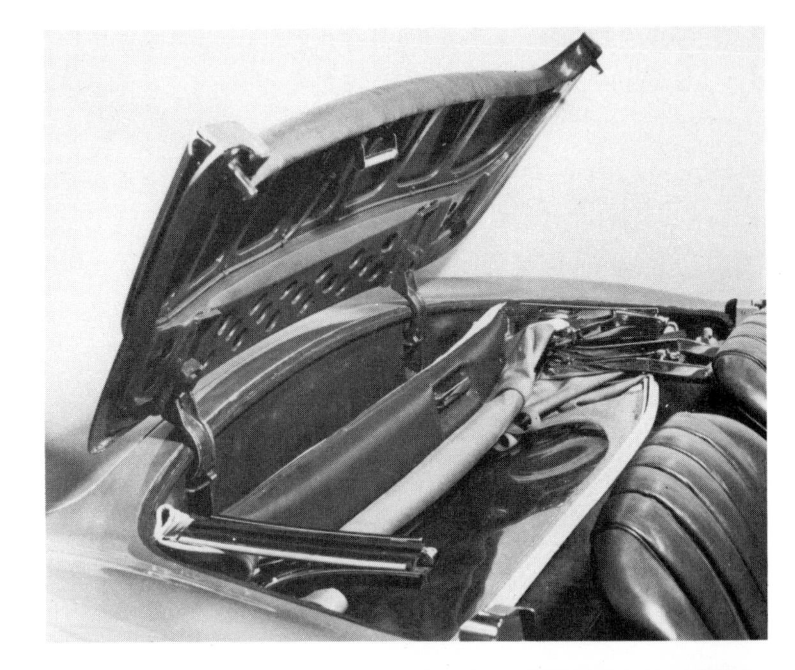

The 300 SL Roadster

A rare combination: outstanding road performance plus luxury

The new 300 SL Roadster bears a very close design kinship to the highly successful 300 SLR competition sports car and the 2.5 liter W 196 Mercedes-Benz Grand Prix car. The addition of compensating springs on the 300 SL's single joint rear swing axle results in handling and cornering characteristics of a very high order. Proper use of power and steering will take the 300 SL Roadster through difficult corners at high competition speeds. The space frame is redesigned to accommodate conventional doors, and flexibility of the 250 hp fuel injection engine is such that *smooth* acceleration from 15 mph in top gear to maximum speed is easily achieved. Actual overall performance of the 300 SL Roadster is what you would expect: *Outstanding!*

However, what you would not ordinarily expect in a car of such high performance are the luxurious seats and appointments you find in the 300 SL Roadster. Roll-up windows and a snug, truly all-weather top that goes up in seconds, extremely comfortable leather bucket seats and a redesigned instrument nacelle for instant reading are some of the features.

Mercedes-Benz motor cars are distributed exclusively in the U. S. by the Studebaker-Packard Corporation and are sold and serviced by Studebaker-Packard dealers.

100 mph not to be exceeded for the first 300 miles, or 125 mph for the following 600 miles, after which, they had been assured, it was permissible to gradually improve on these speeds, towards the normal maximum. Nevertheless, the two 300SL coupés contrived to put 210 miles into the first three hours running, in spite of lorries that drew into their path, icy patches on the motorway, and the onset of darkness. The next day their journey was resumed, from Aachen to Ostend, Jack passing Rob at some 140 mph when he himself was cruising at about two-miles-a-minute in the rain, which Walker

Left *An interesting reminder that in the States the Studebaker-Packard Corporation acted as distributors for the Mercedes-Benz 300SL*

Back-axle details showing development changes (see text)

found very impressive—until his car was covered in spray. . . . The average for the final 50 miles of this return home from the Continent was done at 100 mph. Incidentally, I remarked earlier that special colours were available for 300SLs, to option. Rob's had been painted red, but he later had it painted white, and blue underneath, like his other 300SL, which he said made it look smaller and lower. . . .

A hard-top for the normally soft-hooded 300SL Roadster

The next important development in 300SL evolution was the advent of the Roadster, which made its debut at the Geneva Motor Show in March 1957. It replaced the coupé 300SL as a production model, and it incorporated several important improvements. In fact, the former closed gull-wing car was not made after 1956. The new Roadster was regarded as a cabriolet in America, because it had a

Overleaf *A comparison in Roadsters. Lightweight on the left?*

S-AP 184
BB-K 56

disappearing hood and wind-up side windows. It was a very acceptable extension of the 300SL theme, and production went from 1957 until it was run down six years later, a total of 1858 300SL Roadsters being made, or some 458 more than that of the coupé.

Conscious of the shortcomings of the original swing-axle of the coupé, the D-B engineers evolved a low-pivot version for the Roadster, to ensure that it handled better. Dunlop disc brakes were provided for it, on all its wheels, from March 1961. With lower tubular framework at the rear of the chassis and a third compensator coil-spring to reduce rear-end roll stiffness and further improve road-holding, this openable 300SL Roadster was an impressive car. It retained the same purposeful appearance as the coupé, including the side ventilator-vanes, but a smaller fuel tank that wrapped round the spare

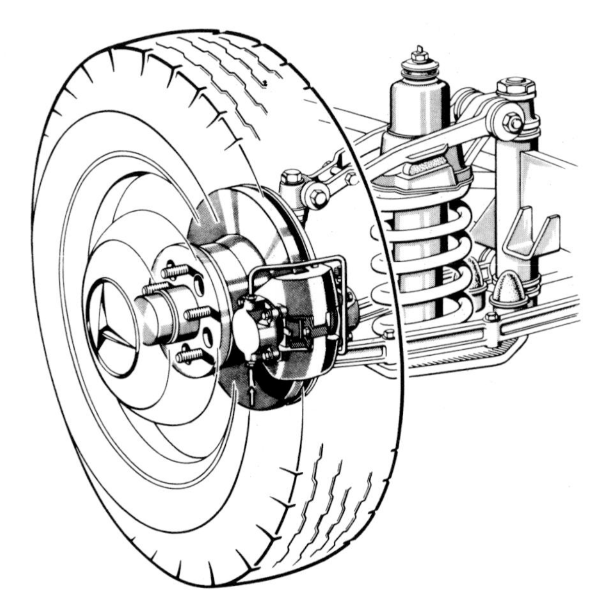

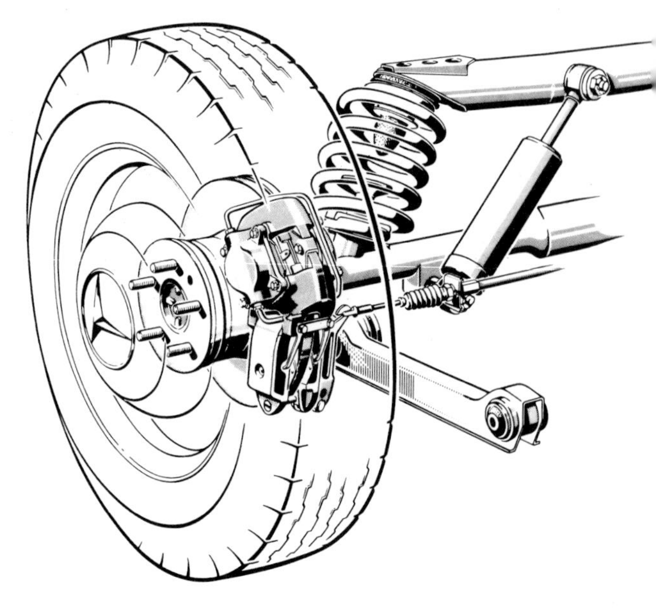

*The front suspension (*left*) and rear suspension arrangements of the 300SL with the later disc brakes fitted*

wheel enabled luggage to be stowed in a proper boot with lift-up lid, and the hood stowed away in another compartment behind the two bucket seats. The doors were normal, front-hinged ones, possible because of the lower rear-frame structure. The Roadster was heavier than the coupé by about 200 lb and its track was wider, although the wheelbase remained the same.

There had been a somewhat similar-looking open sports two-seater Mercedes-Benz, the 190SL Roadster, introduced alongside the first 300SL. It used the four-cylinder 1897 cc overhead camshaft engine and cost £2896 in England in 1958, its top speed being about 109 mph, and 0–60 mph acceleration taking 13.3 seconds. It may have whetted some appetites for the exciting 300SL Roadster. The latter had a maximum speed of 138 mph at 6000 rpm in the 3.89:1 top gear and it would accelerate from rest to 60 mph in 7.8 seconds. That was on the lowest of five available axle-ratios.

The 300SL Roadster was not intended for racing but a special lightweight edition was used by O'Shea and Tilp for 1957 competitions in the USA. It won Class D in the SCCA championship, its dependability helping when its speed was outclassed by the current Ferrari and Maserati sports/racing jobs.

Overleaf *A Roadster prepared for competition work with roll-cage, as required for racing in America. The factory's only specially prepared competition open car on the 300SL chassis*

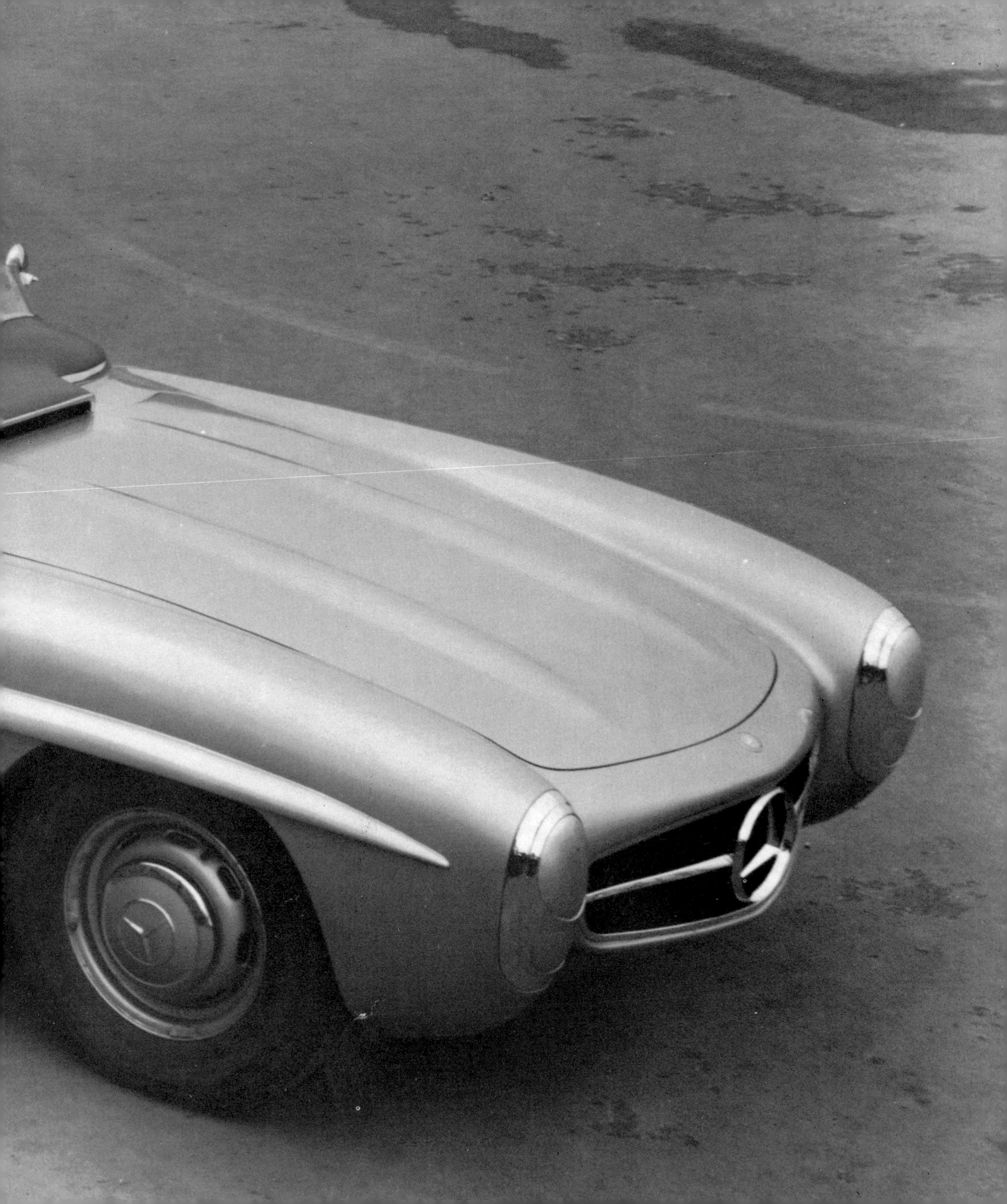

Chapter 5
The spin off

Peak sports-racing achievement. Top *The magnificent straight-eight, fuel-injection, desmodromically-valved 300SLR engine of the Mercedes-Benz and,* bottom, *the astonishing car with the body removed. Note the inboard drum brakes in the top illustration*

All the experimenting and research that Daimler-Benz had put into the 300SL were really only a lead-up to their return to international motor-racing in 1954. For this enthralling project the fabulous 300SLR sports/racing cars were evolved, but the prime target was Grand Prix racing, with the W196 single-seaters. Such racing is outside the scope of this book and the 300SLR sports/racing cars were similar technically to the GP cars. Both were convincingly to re-establish the three-pointed star of Mercedes-Benz as invincible on the circuits.

The 300SLR had a 78×78 mm (2982 cc) straight-eight roller-bearing engine with desmodromic valve-gear and fuel-injection, now tilted to the off-side of the car. The initial power output was an impressive 282 bhp at 7700 rpm, but by 1955, using a straight air-intake ram-pipe, peak power rose to 302 bhp at 7500 rpm. Limited to 7000 rpm in long races, this magnificent power-unit developed 276 bhp. The chassis borrowed much from the 300SL in the matter of suspension and braking, but the space frame was special to the 300SLR. Altered, too, so that bodywork details would comply with AI sports-car race-regulations. Drum brakes were retained, inboard at front and back, supplemented by air-flap braking for Le Mans. There was even a button for

Top *A first appearance of the soon-to-be-triumphant 300SLR*
Bottom *Stirling Moss explains the practice accident he had with a 300SL coupé while training for the 1955 Mille Miglia. He made up for this, and a practice crash in a 300SLR, by convincingly winning the race*

Opposite top *The driver and navigator before the start of that historic and memorable race and, below, on their way to victory*

722

Over a quarter of a century after their Mille Miglia victory Moss and Jenkinson meet again, at the opening of new Mercedes-Benz showrooms in Picadilly, London. And with typical Daimler-Benz efficiency the 300SLR they drove (slightly modified) had come from the Stuttgart Museum
Right *A flashback to the sad 1955 Le Mans race which the 300 SLRs were leading when withdrawn*

the driver, whereby he could squirt oil on a locking brake!

Rudolf Uhlenhaut naturally had a road-going 300SLR coupé, and this was tried by the intrepid Gordon Wilkins in 1957. He got 180 mph from it, and 136 mph (at 8000 rpm) in the fourth speed of the 5-speed gearbox. The axle ratio was 3.48:1. Using a 3.81 back end 0–60 mph took a mere 6.8 seconds, using only first and second. The engine was giving 296 bhp at 7450 rpm and it was found possible to average 120 mph from Milan to Como. . . . But no

DUNLOP
SPICER
26
20
21
19

Opposite *A splendid shot of a 300SLR on the way to victory in the 1955 Targa Florio race in Sicily; note the Mercedes flag at the roadside*

Below *That startling air brake in action, at Le Mans*

300SLR was ever sold to the public, although two of the coupés were built, both properly upholstered within. Another interesting vehicle was the Mercedes-Benz racing car transporter for the W196 GP cars. It was powered by a 300SL engine and would do just about 100 mph with one racing car on board.

The 300SLR made its debut in the 1955 Mille Miglia 1000-mile road race in Italy. It is now history that Stirling Moss won after a tremendous ten-hour dice, averaging nearly 98 mph, navigated by Denis Jenkinson and his roller-map of the course. In practice they had crashed one 'training' 300SLR and a 300SL coupé, by the way. At least eight private owners of 300SL Mercedes-Benz turned up

106

D
15

in Brescia to support the 300SLR team. Then, in a 130-mile race in Sweden, the 300SLRs of Fangio and Moss were 1st and 2nd, Fangio averaging 99.72 mph.

At Le Mans in 1955 came the terrible accident when Levegh's 300SLR plunged into the crowd (he had been given the drive in a Mercedes-Benz as a token of respect after his heroic failure in 1952) and the other cars from Stuttgart were withdrawn—when in a winning situation. In the TT race in Ulster the three 300SLRs came home 1, 2, 3, in the order Moss/Fitch, Fangio/Kling and von Trips/Simon/Kling, the winning Mercedes averaging 88.32 mph. With Moss and Collins then winning the Targa Florio in a 300SLR at 59.8 mph, with the Fangio/Kling 300SLR in second place, ahead of the Ferrari challenge, Mercedes-Benz took the 1955 World's Sports-Car Championship with their very advanced and impeccably-prepared cars.

Above *The interior of the rare 300SLR coupé, as used for high-speed commuting by Uhlenhaut, belies the extremely high performance of this great car*

Opposite top *The 300SLR straight-eight coupé, not to be confused with the 'softer' 300SL—the exhaust outlets at the side will be noted*

Opposite bottom *Mercedes-Benz 300SLR enlivens the Silverstone paddock*

As a reward for his performances in Mercedes-Benz GP and sports/racing cars, when Fangio came to London late in 1957 the Mercedes Benz Company presented him with a 300SL Roadster.

Having thus shown yet again their complete superiority in GP and sports-car racing, the great German firm, makers, in my opinion, of the best-engineered motor cars in the world, retired from racing. Down the years Mercedes have made all manner of great automobiles, but in the realms of production sports-cars, none ranks higher than the 300SL, which today is a collector's piece, or a very fine way of enjoying what is left of the open road—depending on your point of view.

Those who could not afford a 300SL or felt their driving-skill would not do it justice could bask in reflected glory with a 1.9-litre four-cylinder 190SL Roadster

Specifications

300SL coupé (Production version)

Engine Six cylinders, 85×88 mm, 2996 cc, 8.5:1 compression-ratio. Overhead camshaft driven by chain, operating two valves per cylinder through finger tappets. Bosch fuel-injection. Seven bearing crankshaft. Dry sump lubrication. Coil ignition. Pump cooling. Valve timing, standard camshaft: Inlet valves open 57 degrees btdc, close 99 degrees after bdc, exhaust valves open 55 degrees btdc, close 29 degrees after tdc: Sports camshaft: Inlet valves open 59 degrees btdc, close 97 degrees abdc, exhaust valves open 74 degrees bbdc, close 36 degrees atdc. Normal maximum power output: 190 bhp (250 SAE hp). Maximum sustained rev limit: 6000 rpm. Maximum safe engine speed, 6400 rpm. Maximum torque: 207 lb ft at 5000 rpm. 8.3:1 compression-ratio.
Clutch Single-dry-plate type.
Gearbox Four forward speeds and reverse. Central gear-lever, cranked back on the first 55 production cars, then from early 1955 short lever with remote linkage.
Axle-ratio Choice of 3.64, 3.25, 3.42, 3.89 and 4.11 to 1.
Normal gear-ratios
Tyre-size 6.70×15. (Continental or Dunlop.)
Chassis Space frame of small-diameter steel tubing.
Suspension Front: Independent, with dual wishbones and coil springs. Rear: Swing-axle independent, with coil springs.
Brakes Drum brakes. Hydraulic operation, with mechanical linkage for hand-brake on rear drums. Drum size, 260 mm×90 mm (wide); Al-Fin type with cast-aluminium shoes having cemented-on Ferodo VG95 linings. Two leading shoes at front, leading and trailing shoes at rear. $1\frac{1}{8}$ in. operating cylinders front, and rear; $\frac{1}{16}$ in. rear operating cylinders on most cars. Treadle-Vac suction servo assistance, changed in 1955 to a ATE T50 vacuum-servo.
Wheelbase 94.6 in.

Track Front, 54.6 in., Rear, 56.5 in.
Length 178.1 in.
Width 70.5 in.
Height 51.2 in.
Turning circle 37 ft 4.7 in.
Weight Empty, 2557 lb. Kerb weight, full tank: Approx. 2880 lb. Chassis weight, 181 lb.
Wheels Bolt-on disc or Rudge-type centre-lock wire. 5½K rims.
Body Gull-wing coupé of steel panels with alloy bonnet, doors and rear deck. All-aluminium body available, reducing weight by 176 lb.
Fuel system Electric fuel-feed. 34.3 gallon tank. Fuel filler on off-side. Fuel pressure: 570–680 lb sq. in.
Weight distribution Approx. 48/52 per cent front-rear.
Capacities Coolant: 26.9 qt. Engine oil: 11.7 qt. Battery, 12 volt, 56 amp-hr.
Steering Recirculating-ball. Ratio: 17.3 to 1. Hinged steering wheel Left-hand drive.
British price (1955) £4651.
Performance 0–50 mph in 4.7 sec, 0–70 mph in 8.5 sec, 0–100 mph in 16.1 sec, on the 3.64:1 axle ratio, giving indirect gear ratios of 12.3, 7.17 and 5.04 to 1. Top speed: 125 to 175 mph approx., depending on axle ratio. Fuel consumption: approx. 15 mpg.
Production period 1954 to 1957.
Production breakdown 1954, 146: 1955, 867: 1956, 300: 1957, 76. Total: 1440, of which 29 were the Lightweight model.

300SL Roadster

As coupé except
Suspension Low-pivot swing axle, at rear, with compensating coil spring.
Brakes 11.43 in. diameter Dunlop disc brakes.
Track 55.1 in. front, 57.1 in. rear.
Length 180.1 in.
Tyres 5.70 × 15.
Fuel tank 26.4 gallons.
Weight Kerb weight, 3040 lb. With hard-top: 3220 lb.
Production run 1957 to 1963.
Production breakdown 1957, 554: 1958, 324: 1959, 211: 1960, 249: 1961, 250: 1962, 244: 1963, 26. Total, 1858.
NB The sports camshaft was fitted to all Roadsters.

Acknowledgements

Great hospitality and considerable help were given by Daimler-Benz Aktiengesellschaft (Abt. Archiv—Geschichfe—Museum) at Stuttgart. Nothing was too much trouble for them. Others contributed successfuly for all concerned; the author's collection, Karl Ludvigsen Collection, LAT, Tim Parker, the late Jerry Ames, the late George Monkhouse, and Rodolfo Mailander. Then there was the Mercedes-Benz Owners Club (GB) and M-B dealers Rose and Young of Caterham; Jerry Porter, Mr Cushway and Mr Bellamy both who loaned their cars; and Gerald Foster who shot the car of James A. Douglass in Newport Beach.

Mirco Decet did all the leg work and much of the photography.

Index

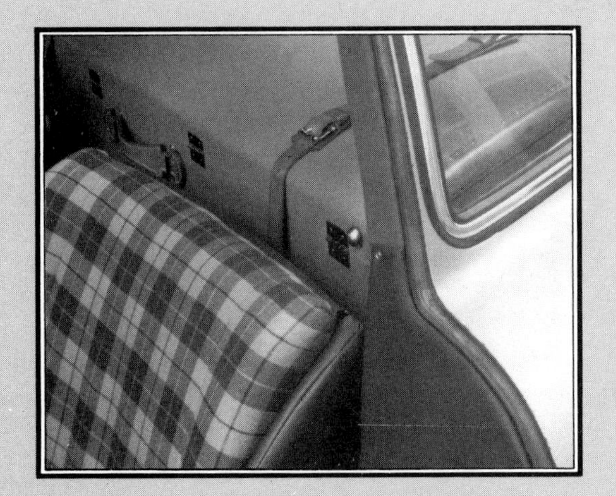